egg decorating

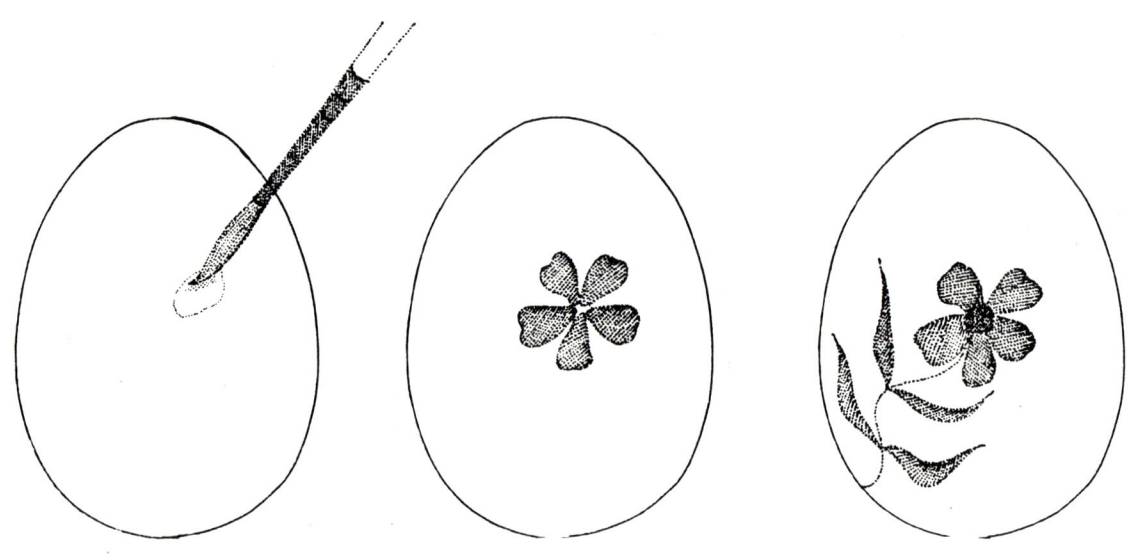

egg decorating
Louise Riotte

Drake Publishers Inc.
New York

Published in 1973 by
Drake Publishers Inc.
381 Park Avenue South
New York, N.Y. 10016

All rights reserved. No portion of this book may be reproduced without written permission from the publisher.

Library of Congress Catalog Card Number 72-10494
ISBN 0-87749-417-7

Printed in Italy

Prepared and produced for the publisher by BMG Productions, Incorporated

Photographs by Louise Riotte
Book Design by Elaine Gongora

Contents

Foreword

Author's Preface

CHAPTER ONE Beautiful Eggs with Humble Materials	1
CHAPTER TWO Blossoming Eggs	9
CHAPTER THREE Rose-Scented Eggs	17
CHAPTER FOUR Jeweled Eggs for All Occasions	23
CHAPTER FIVE Jeweled Eggs of the Zodiac	37
CHAPTER SIX Egghead Eggs	43
CHAPTER SEVEN Leather-Clad Western Eggs	53
CHAPTER EIGHT Cutting the Eggshells	69

CHAPTER NINE 77
Eggs on the Half Shell

CHAPTER TEN 93
Colors, Paints, and Finishes

CHAPTER ELEVEN 103
Make Your Own Egg Stands

CHAPTER TWELVE 109
Eggs That Bloom in the Spring

CHAPTER THIRTEEN 119
Decorating with German Scrap

CHAPTER FOURTEEN 127
The Eggshells and I

CHAPTER FIFTEEN 137
From Fun to Fabulous

CHAPTER SIXTEEN 161
The Insides of the Eggs

Suppliers 171
Index 174

Foreword

This book is lovingly dedicated by an "all thumbs" writer to her "all thumbs" readers who want to try their hands at the fascinating craft of egg decoration.

This is an idea book as well as a how-to book, meant to trigger your imagination so that you may create designs of your own.

In it you will find ways of decorating eggs with materials for which you need go no further than your own backyard and which cost absolutely nothing. You'll also find eggs for which expensive materials are used, even brilliants and braid. There are "country cousin" eggs which require no more than a bit of cotton print, a few candles, and rickrack from the dimestore. There are unusual eggs, such as those decorated with German "scrap," a versatile material very popular years ago with our grandmothers but seldom heard of today. You'll discover leather-clad Westerners and velvet-clad aristocrats, eggs for special occasions, Easter and Christmas, Halloween and Valentine Day—even a mischievous leprechaun for Saint Patrick's. And how about a bassinet for a baby shower? Or an egg that's just the beautiful right size when used as a decoration on top of a cake? Some of the decorated eggs I will tell you about will have a pearly sheen, others will glow softly in the dark. Would you believe that some are even fragrant?

Instructions for making your own egg stands are included. So are amusing "eggheads" which require only scraps of fake fur, tiny plastic champagne glasses, acrylic paint, etc. There's even a fun way to paint pictures with all the eggshells an "all thumbs" egg decorator has broken along the way. And there's a cookwagon chapter on how to use up the insides of those dozens of eggs that have been decorated on the outside —you don't have to scramble and eat *all* of them.

My fondest hope is that children of all ages will find something here that will appeal to them.

Author's Preface

Elegance in egg decoration probably reached its zenith between 1883 and 1917, for it was during these years that Peter Carl Fabergé, at the request of the Russian tsars, designed and produced 57 Imperial Easter eggs, each one more beautiful than the last. These exquisite eggs have never been surpassed and only rarely equalled.

Each egg, executed in jewels and precious metals, contained a surprise in some way complimentary to the Empress Alexandra Feodorovna or the Dowager Empress Marie, for whom they were designed twice a year—at Easter and at Christmas.

But these eggs, lovely as they were, are representative of only a small part of the history of decorating eggs. Eggs have been cherished by many peoples in many lands, been decorated in various ways, and given as gifts to families and friends.

The ancient Persians speak of "Ormuzd, born of pure light," who produced, among other wonders, "twenty-four gods, who were put into an egg." An extravagant fantasy, of course, but it points to the fact that since the very beginning of time eggs have played an important role and received all due respect. The ancient Egyptians, the Greeks, and the Romans also exchanged decorated eggs with each other.

Eggs symbolize life and hope, here and now, and many peoples have renewed their faith in these ideas by eating eggs, dyeing them (in various colors, most often red), and giving them as presents to one another at the festival of the New Year, celebrated at the spring equinox.

Man very early perceived the egg as the one perfect thing in the universe, encasing the germ of life in a container that is pleasing to both touch and sight. Early Christians looked upon the egg as symbolic of the Resurrection. The Chinese regarded the egg as a symbol of life. Friends and relatives, upon the birth of a child, looked forward to the distribution of red-colored eggs which were considered appropriate for the occasion.

But Easter which is, of course, a Christian festival, is probably the time of year when eggs receive the most attention. Perhaps one of the reasons for this is because in the springtime of the year eggs are likely to be most plentiful.

History records that the early Christians of Mesopotamia were the first to dye eggs and exchange them with each other and, in time, the delightful custom spread.

In England, friends often wrote messages and dates on the eggs they exchanged. In Germany, where eggs are often hand-painted in traditional patterns, an old verse, possibly a special family poem, was often carefully printed on the eggs.

Candy eggs, elaborately fashioned with a window at one end and tiny scenes inside, were popular gifts in the 1800s. (Egg molds to make these fascinating, scenic, panorama or chocolate eggs are still available. They come in three sizes: tiny, $3^{1}/_{8} \times 2^{1}/_{8} \times 2$ inches; medium, $4^{1}/_{4} \times 3 \times 3$ inches; and large, $5^{1}/_{4} \times 4 \times 4$ inches, and may be purchased from Maid of Scandinavia (see suppliers' listing).

Even today, children love to find chocolate, plastic, or even cardboard eggs filled with candy waiting for them at the breakfast table on Easter morning, or hidden along with the real ones, when they go egg hunting.

My parents were German and when I was a child, I was told the legend of the Easter hare who "brings pretty eggs to good children," which I firmly believed. How this story began is very charming.

It seems that a poor woman dyed some eggs during a famine and hid them in a nest as an Easter gift for her children. Just as the children discovered the nest a rabbit leaped away and the children thought the rabbit had brought the eggs. This charming story spread and since it so delighted the youngsters, it eventually grew into an Easter legend.

In ancient Egypt, the rabbit, or hare, symbolized birth and new life. Some ancient people considered it a symbol of the moon. It became an Easter symbol, possibly because the moon determines the date of Easter.

Back in the year A.D. 325, the Christian fathers held the Council of

Nicea at which the date of Easter was definitely settled and this ruling is still kept today. They decided that Easter should be celebrated on the first Sunday after the full moon following the twenty-first day of March. And so it came about that the rabbit, or hare, became associated with the Easter festival.

Many customs connected with the Easter season have come down from pagan festivals of spring. Others stem from the Passover celebration. The name for Easter in some languages comes from the Hebrew "Pesah." The Italians call Easter Pasqua; the Spaniards, Pascua; and the French, Paques.

The word "Easter," itself, quite probably derives from Eostre, the Anglo-Saxon goddess of spring. Years ago children in Germany believed that the stork, the fox and the cuckoo brought them eggs at *Ostern* (pronounced OH-stern).

The Ethiopians also had their Easter customs. During Lent, regarded by Christians as a time of self-denial and penance, no one ate meat, butter, milk or eggs. The evening before Easter, the parents and children customarily attended a church service that ended at three o'clock in the morning. After this was over, they returned to their homes to rest and celebrate with elaborate food, eggs being a special treat.

People in Ireland dance on Easter day to win prize cakes and break the long fast of Lent by eating eggs at dawn on Easter Sunday.

In Belgium and France, mothers sometimes tell their children that the Easter chimes bring their eggs. And Belgian children like to make nests of hay and hide them in the grass for the Easter bunny to fill. Also, in France and some other European countries, church bells do not ring from Good Friday to Easter. One legend has it that the bells fly to Rome until Easter, and drop eggs on the way back for boys and girls to find.

In Germany, eggs are colored green on Green Thursday (Maundy Thursday) and the people carry them about all day for good luck.

Easter Monday is celebrated by the young people with an egg-rolling contest called "Eierlesen" and the winner gets a prize of 101 Easter eggs. My father also told me of a custom in his village called "cracking the eggs." Two children would each hold an Easter egg upright and hit the two eggs against each other. If only one egg cracked and the other remained firm, the winner was given the cracked egg to eat. If both cracked, each one had a small feast.

In Italy, a priest blesses the Easter eggs before the holiday. Housewives place eggs at the center of the Easter table, and arrange other foods around them. A moderately well-to-do family may have as many as two hundred brightly colored eggs in the centerpiece.

In the Netherlands, young and old both play games on Easter Monday involving eggs. During Holy Week (the week before Easter) children collect the eggs by going from door to door with a basket.

Children in Finland indulge in the quaint custom of beating the adults with the gaily trimmed "Lenten birches," performing this ritual on Holy Saturday and receiving Easter Eggs in "payment."

Young people in Hungary also have a strange custom, for on Easter Monday the boys sprinkle the girls with perfumed water and receive Easter eggs as their "reward."

In Greece and Rumania, people tap red eggs together as an Easter greeting when they meet. One says "Christ is risen," and the other replies, "Truly, He is risen."

On Holy Saturday, the Bulgarians exchange eggs and baked almond cakes that the priest has blessed. In the Ukraine people celebrate Easter for two whole weeks. Many people think the Ukrainian Easter eggs are the most beautiful of all. Each village has its own designs, which may include fir trees, priests' robes, bell towers, and chapels. The Ukrainians often cast eggshells on the waters of streams to show the dead that it is Easter. At one time, Ukranian girls used to make their cheeks glow by rubbing them with eggs dyed red.

In Mexico, a large egg-shaped *piñata,* a jar made of pottery, is filled with candy and hung for the children to break. They make a game out of this, blindfolding one of their number and giving him a long stick. The *piñata,* usually hung over a tree branch on a long cord, is pulled up just out of his reach as he repeatedly strikes at it, accompanied by gales of laughter from the children gathered to watch. When it is finally broken everyone scampers around to pick up his share. Paper and cardboard *piñatas* shaped like rabbits and other Easter symbols are also used.

Though Easter-egg rolling is a custom practiced in many countries, probably the most famous takes place on the White House lawn in Washington, D.C. Every year thousands of adults and children, guests of the First Lady of the land, gather to roll Easter eggs on the lawn on the Monday following Easter Sunday. The custom was started in 1879 by President Hayes and, except between the years 1943 and 1953, has been observed ever since.

But, wonderful as the Easter eggs and customs are, almost as many eggs are decorated now for Christmas and other holidays. We shall explore some of these ideas more fully later on.

egg decorating

CHAPTER ONE

Beautiful Eggs with Humble Materials

With so much attention being paid to ecology it seems fitting to begin with eggs which can be decorated with materials that are of natural origin, and that we can find in our own backyard.

The decorations for these eggs have the added attraction of costing absolutely nothing, and even young children can participate in the fun. I believe the custom of using onion skins (the thin, brown, dry skins that slip off as the onions dry) originated in Germany. I remember how much I looked forward to Easter as a child so that I could have the fun of helping in the preparation of the eggs.

Since we had a garden, we always had our own onion skins, carefully saved during the winter months. From time to time, as the skins dried and turned brown, we would slip them off and place them in a mesh bag (using one of fairly close weave so small particles would not be lost) and hang them where the air could reach them so further drying could take place.

Those years that we had a good supply of both yellow and red onions, the skins of the two different colors were saved separately as each would give a different tint to the eggs. If we did not have enough of either one we cooked them together and the results were still attractive.

As a little girl I had been told the legend of the Easter rabbit (or hare) and I accepted, without question, the eggs that I found on Easter morning, carefully hidden about the yard, as a gift left from him. As I grew older I was told that I could assist with the egg coloring on Easter Sunday because "the rabbit needed help," and I was thus led by gentle stages into reality.

This did not lessen but rather added to my joy at Easter time, for now my mother and I worked together coloring the eggs for friends and egg hunts at the church and school. I was beginning to feel very grown up.

While my mother was busy in the kitchen making a broth from onion skins, I would take my basket and go out to the yard and the fields around our home and search for flowers and leaves and grasses.

Spring comes early in southern Oklahoma where I now live, and there was always an abundance of flowers from which to choose, especially the tiny flowers which look the best. Among our favorites were spring beauties (or the Indian name, "Miskodeed"), five-petaled white flowers with fine pin stripes of rose, and the lovely, all-white Star of Bethlehem. Violets, japonica, small dandelions, grape hyacinths, redbud, and small roses also went into my basket, along with several sprays of Indian paintbrush.

As I hunted, I would also take note of the fine, fernlike leaves of young yarrow plants, clover leaves (and what fun it was to find an occasional four-leaved one), and real ferns, if I could find them, growing in mossy places beside the brook.

Nor did I overlook the decorative possibilities of dried grasses, still to be found in corners here and there, left over from winter and still holding their shape. Weeds of all sorts, with interesting outlines, came in for a great deal of attention, for some of these make markings on the eggs as pretty as the cultivated flowers and plants.

When I returned with my treasure I would find my mother seated at the kitchen table busily tearing an old sheet or pillow slip into long strips, about an inch wide and a yard or so long. This old material, washed many times and worn thin, had been put away sometime during the year and saved especially for this day.

It was not only a good way to get a last bit of use from the sheet instead of discarding it, but my mother knew from long experience that this thin, soft material would work far better than new yard goods. If the material was strong enough selvedges would be torn into strips about $1/4$ of an inch wide. If not, she would have a spool of thin, soft white twine ready to use for tying the wider cloth securely after the eggs were wrapped.

The first Easter that I "helped the rabbit" was probably the most

Placing natural materials on uncooked egg.

exciting of all and I was eager to learn how the eggs were colored. My mother placed a large, soft bath towel on the table, and cautioned me to hold the egg I was wrapping over this.

Next she showed me how to take a bit of flower or fern and place it directly on the egg, laying it as flat as possible so the imprint would be clear and definite.

As each bit of flower or fern was laid against the egg, the cloth was pulled over it and firmly held, then another flower would be put on, continuing in this manner until the egg was completely covered, giving a half-turn twist to the cloth when I had gone around the egg once, so that each end would be covered after placing a flower or leaf on each.

Of course, I was not able to cover the egg completely with flowers, nor is it desirable to do so, for the contrasting brown is what makes the eggs pretty, but I was told to put on as much as I could.

After the egg was completely wrapped with the inch-wide strip of cloth I was shown how gently to tighten the wrappings by going over all once more with the narrow cloth or twine (even coarse thread can be used), so that the covering would not come off in the coloring bath.

Then came the best part. The onion skin broth, having been cooled to room temperature, was again placed over a low fire and the wrapped eggs placed in the broth. It is not necessary to remove the onion skins when this is done.

I should mention here that the eggs themselves had been removed from the refrigerator the night before so they could warm to room temperature. They color better if they are not cold and there is also less chance that they will crack and undo all your work.

Make sure the eggs are well covered in the broth and do not try to put in too many at one time. For a four-quart saucepan three to five eggs at one time is all you should try to cook. After the eggs have been placed in the broth, you simply cook them just as you would any hard-cooked eggs.

In cooking the eggs I like to place them in the broth and heat it rather slowly, letting them simmer for a full eight minutes so the shells will take up as much color as possible.

When the time is up, take the eggs out one at a time with a large slotted spoon, flicking any onion skins that may cling back into the saucepan. Place the eggs in water that is at room temperature, and allow them to cool until they can be conveniently handled.

After a few minutes you can change the water to cool the eggs more rapidly if you are in a hurry, or have two pans handy and just slip them into the other one.

By now the wrappings should begin to slip off easily but if necessary, untie them, pull off the cloth and discard. (If you are pressed for materials you can rinse them out in clear water, hang them up to dry and reuse.)

Taking off the wrappings is always the most exciting part of this egg technique and I am still just as eager as I was as a child to see what has taken place. Did the violets print off purple? The japonica rose? Did the fern markings come out clearly? Sometimes this happens, but not always. The yellow of the dandelion or the blue of the grape hyacinth may leave its color on the eggs, but green and yellow prints usually predominate on the eggs.

No matter how many of these eggs you make—and perhaps this is one reason I find these eggs so fascinating—every one will be different, a completely creative effort unlike any other—unique.

As you work with these eggs and become more adept at the wrapping procedure, you may want to try for different effects, all violets, all pansies, or even the delicate fern tracery. I have found, after doing these for many years, that colors vary from one year to the next in the same blossoms, possibly depending on moisture content at the time of picking.

You will also find that there may be a variation in the eggshells themselves depending on the lime content of the shell; some eggs will be a deeper, richer brown than others.

After the wrappings have been removed, place the eggs on a couple of layers of absorbent paper towels to dry thoroughly. Then, while they are still warm, add a bit of glamor by rubbing them with cooking oil (I prefer Crisco as it is not sticky) with a soft cloth. You will find that this will further enhance the beauty of the coloring as it deepens and brightens the design color and the brown or reddish-brown background.

These eggs, with their lovely, shadowy imprints, are especially pretty if mixed in baskets with brightly colored "plain" eggs. The reds, blues, greens, purples, and yellows emphasize and complement the unusual brown eggs and make them seem lovelier and more interesting by contrast.

There are several more things to know about the "flower" eggs. You can, if you wish, write names on them with a wax pencil instead of or in combination with the flowers before cooking them in the broth.

You can also cut out small pictures of thin cardboard or heavy paper and wrap them on the eggs along with the grasses or leaves. Tiny rabbits and chicks are special favorites.

Any size eggs can be decorated in this manner, but I prefer white chicken eggs, as large as I can get them, as they are easier to handle and afford more surface for the decoration.

These eggs are so easy that, once started, you will probably want to have a great many—some to decorate your table with and some for the children to put in their baskets. You need not have any qualms whatever about letting the youngsters enjoy them. Even if the egg should crack in the cooking process and a bit of the brown gets on the egg, it is perfectly harmless.

It is also good to know that the eggs can be made several days in advance of the time when they will be needed. After they have been cooked you can simply return them to the egg carton and store them in the refrigerator. They will keep just as well as any other hard-cooked eggs. The oil film may dull a little when the eggs are cold, but it will quickly become glossy again when they are taken out and returned to room temperature.

Depending on the part of the world you live in, there are many other natural materials that can be used for coloring eggs. Some people use beet juice or even coffee grounds. In Russia the *Pasque* flower,

Anemone pulsatilla, which imparts a green color, has been used to color Paschal or Easter eggs. In England, furze or gorse, a shrub with yellow flowers, has been used.

Another way of using this tie-and-dye method if you intend to use the eggs for decorative purposes only (I would not recommend that these ever be eaten) is to use Rit or Putnam dye, following the directions on the package as you would if you were going to dye a garment.

If you plan to use Rit you simply prepare the Rit solution in a basin or the sink by straining the dissolved dye solution into hot tap water. This will give you light pastel colors. However, to bring out the true value of the color, I prefer to prepare the Rit solution in a pan on the stove by straining the dissolved dye solution into simmering water.

Prepare the eggs for dyeing just as you would for putting them in the onion skin broth. Be sure that they are perfectly clean, with no oil or grease on them to prevent even coloring.

I always get better results if I wet the cloth wrappings of the eggs before placing them in the dye solution. Since these eggs are not to be eaten, I simmer them in the dye solution for 15 or 20 minutes so the color will be deep and rich.

Also, the manufacturer recommends that you use about three gallons of water for each package of Rit. I prefer to use two gallons or even less. If the eggs come out darker than you like you can always add more water after you look at the first ones.

Here, again, you will have to experiment a little, because, as I said before, the color absorption of the egg shells will vary.

Remember, too, that if you want only a few eggs of each color you do not have to use the entire package of dye. You can make a strong solution by using half of a package (about $1^1/_3$-tablespoon) of dye for about a quart of water. For this I would suggest that you put the solution in a container large enough to avoid overcrowding and dye only one or two eggs at a time.

As with the "onion skin" coloring, I always have the eggs at room temperature for this operation and I also let the dye solution cool before placing the eggs in it, bringing it up to simmering just as I did for the other eggs.

These eggs also will be more beautiful if a slight film of oil is applied to them while they are still slightly warm. If you are wondering about their perishable qualities I can only draw on my own experience. One year I made some of these eggs and they were just too pretty to throw away. I kept putting it off (I should mention that none of them were cracked), and finally I wrapped each one separately and put them all in

Eggs colored with onion skins displayed on antique Mexican scale.

a box, meaning to store them away for a short time to see what would happen.

As luck would have it, other incidents occurred which completely erased the eggs from my mind and I did not find them until several months later when I was rummaging around looking for something else. I pulled out the box and took it outdoors, expecting the worst.

Actually I was surprised. Apparently the contents had simply dried up inside the egg—when I shook them, there was a rattling sound inside. And there was no offensive odor. I carefully rewrapped the eggs and was able to use them again, along with new ones in new colors, at a later date.

Speaking of using the eggs for decoration, there are lots of other ideas besides just putting them in a basket. I like to vary my centerpiece for the table at Easter time from year to year. Once I even used my little son's battered dump truck to his great delight, placing it on a wooden board and pouring sand around it. The truck was filled with the flower eggs and a lot of them were nested in the sand which kept them from rolling around. If you have young children, such an arrangement would probably delight them more than any other.

For something more sophisticated I once used a pair of antique scales, handmade of beaten and polished brass, which I found some years ago while on a trip to Mexico. These scales, set on a round mirror with fresh spring flowers around their base, were a delight to both family and friends.

I'm a born "saver" and another arrangement involved the pretty shells the children and I picked up on a vacation trip to Galveston, Texas. They reminded all of us of the happy time we had digging them out of the sand and playing on the beach. Shells and eggs were placed together in a low bowl of deep ruby red, which I placed in the center of the table on a white lace doily.

An old-fashioned stagecoach which served as the base for displaying the eggs is another of my happy Easter memories. The dark cranberry pottery of the coach with its "gold" trim was a perfect foil for the bright eggs which I placed both inside, on the top, and all around. I concealed a tiny bit of florist clay under each egg to hold it in place.

These are only a few ideas and, while you may not have exactly the same materials to use for your decoration you will probably find others around your home just as interesting. It's fun to dare to be different and use something besides the time-honored basket, pretty as it is.

CHAPTER TWO

Blossoming Eggs

There is another fun way to decorate eggs with natural materials which is almost as inexpensive as coloring them in the onion-skin broth. These eggs may be left white, brown, or colored according to your fancy; they are equally pretty in all shades, depending on the contrasting colors of the flowers and ferns you use.

To get the most enjoyment from working with this type of egg decoration, you should begin planning several months ahead of the time you will want to make them—say, during the winter when you are planning your spring garden.

And, while you may repeatedly experiment with flowers of different types and colors, as I do, it is good to know ahead of time that certain varieties respond better than others to the drying process which this form of decoration requires.

I am fortunate in having several polyantha roses in shades of pink, red, and salmon in my garden. These are the little roses that blossom in clusters and have very small petals. Since I have used these many times, I know they work very well.

Other flowers such as Mexican zinnias, the dwarf French marigolds, dianthus, clematis, shasta daisies, pansies, violas, larkspur, forget-me-nots, baby's breath, bachelor buttons, coral bells, and black-eyed susans are also especially good.

You need not choose all of your flowers merely because they are small; you can cut the petals down a little smaller, change the color of the centers, and even give them leaves which they do not possess in nature, as I often do.

It is also good to know about such sun-resistant flowers as the gazania sunshine hybrids with their sharply defined, almost dazzling colors which retain their crisp freshness and vigor all through the hottest and driest summers. Another desirable flower is the African daisy (*arctotis*), again a sun-loving plant that will do well in dry soil. (Both of these flowers may be obtained from the Park Seed Co., Greenwood, South Carolina 29646).

I am being rather specific about flowers that will—or will not—dry well, for I find that, in general, wild flowers, or even cultivated types which have a great deal of moisture in their petals, such as begonias or certain types of lilies, will not dry well.

It should also be remembered that the time of day and the stage of maturity of the flowers when picked has a bearing on how well they will dry and preserve.

Try not to pick them too early in the morning while they are still covered with dew and, if possible, delay your picking if you have recently had rain. Even days that are excessively moist and humid are not good days for drying and preserving flowers. Try to pick on sunny days—here in my warm climate I try to get the flowers just about noontime, while the blossoms are dry but still fresh.

Of course you do not have to grow all the flowers you will want to use yourself. If you have a friend who likes to grow pansies and violas every spring, she will probably be glad to give you some, as these little flowers blossom so profusely that picking is actually good for them. If they are not picked, they will set seed and stop blooming.

Now, let's assume that we have chosen our flowers, picked them and they are now on the table ready to be put in the drying medium. For this I think I have tried every preparation I ever learned of and I always come back to my white silica sand. It's inexpensive, convenient to purchase, and always, in my opinion, does a good job.

I buy the silica sand at the lumber yard (or call in advance and have it sacked up) in purchases of five to ten pounds, depending on how many flowers I want to preserve. It is generally sold for about five cents a pound and is almost pure white, very fine and dry.

I like to work with large, shallow boxes approximately 10 by 15 inches in size and about three inches high. I begin by filling the box about half full of the silica sand, smoothing it out so that the layer will be fairly even. I lay the flowers on the sand face downward and snip off

Drying flowers and petals in silica sand.

the stems just as close to the flower head as possible.

If I am working with thick, many-petaled flowers, such as the small roses or zinnias, I take them completely apart so that the petals will dry separately.

Leaves, such as clover and small, flat ferns, also go into the box. Leaves with a reddish tinge, or even small autumn leaves, are especially pretty when the time comes to put the flower designs on the eggs.

After I have placed the flowers on the sand, I gently pour more silica sand over them so they will not be disturbed from the positions I have placed them in. A small pitcher is handy for this—the sand is a bit heavy and sometimes comes out of the sack much too quickly if you attempt to cover them by this quicker but potentially disastrous method. I did this once and scattered sand all over.

Fill the box almost to the brim and set it in some convenient place where it will be out of your way for a few days. Drying time depends on a number of factors, principally the moisture contained in the plants you have chosen and the humidity, or lack of it, in the atmosphere.

If you are in a hurry you can put your flowers in a metal pan, bed them down in the silica sand, cover them up, and place them in a low-temperature oven for several hours. Generally, however, I do not go to this extra trouble. I just plan in advance, put the flowers away upstairs and forget them for a few days.

Three to five days is generally sufficient. Janey leaves and marigold petals will usually dry overnight, others may take the full five days.

When you feel the flowers have dried sufficiently, pour the sand off the flowers very slowly. You can use a large strainer if you like, to rescue any tiny ones, such as lantanas, that might be lost in the sand.

When the flowers are exposed, gently pick them from the box and put them in the containers in which you will store them. I like to use pint-size fruit jars. These will largely exclude moisture, are easy to peek through, and store conveniently. If you have only a small space in which to store your preserved flowers you might try using the small glass jars that baby food is sold in. These have a tight seal and are excellent for this purpose.

Very little of the silica sand will cling to your flowers and petals as they are removed but if it does gently shake or brush it off. I find a flat brush about ¼ inch wide the best for this purpose.

Now, let's leave the flowers for a time and see about the preparation of the eggshells. Whether you want them white or colored is a matter of personal preference; they will be lovely either way for these are very, very special eggs. I always do some each way and later on you will see why.

If I decide to color the eggs there are two ways to proceed. You can color the eggs first without blowing out the contents. I think this saves a lot of time and trouble. Not all eggs will take up color evenly, and if you find several that do not, just wash them off and return them to the refrigerator for ordinary use. Generally speaking, eggs that are warmed to room temperature will color best.

Another thing in favor of coloring the eggs before blowing them out is that they will not float and they can be easily rolled around in the container for an even coating. I like to put the coloring material in pint-size fruit jars and add enough water to cover the eggs completely so the dye job will be uniform.

As to the coloring material itself, there are also several ways to handle this. You can use regular Easter egg dye if you like. My personal preference, however, is Cakolor Paste Colors (Maid of Scandinavia).

These exquisite colors come in 21 different shades: royal blue, bakers rose, lemon yellow, Christmas red (there is one called red red which is the same shade but double strength), violet, royal red, scarlet red, leaf green, golden egg yellow, brown, rose pink, orange, copper tone, cherry red (this also comes in "super red"—the same shade but double strength), sky blue, valentine red, mint green (also known as emerald), royal purple, crimson, turquoise and even black.

You may obtain these colors separately in one-ounce jars, or buy a small assortment in a set for a trial run to see if you like them. They are paste colors and should be mixed with warm water. They were originally intended to color cake frostings and so are perfectly harmless for use on eggs.

The depth of color is determined by the amount of paste color you mix with the water and also by the length of time you leave the egg in the color bath. I find the rose pink particularly beautiful in all shades from pastel to very deep.

Now, if you belong to the other school of thought which finds it preferable to blow the contents of the eggs from the shells before coloring, here is how this can be done.

Again, there are two ways to do this. The first is to take room temperature eggs and, using a small nail, large needle, or, as I prefer it, a corsage pin, pierce a small hole in the small end of the egg. Pierce a slightly larger hole in the large end of the egg, moving the pin around inside the egg so you will be sure to break the yolk. Next, either shake or blow the egg contents out into a bowl. Rinse out the egg with cold running water and blow out any that you cannot remove by shaking the egg. Set the egg upright in an egg carton and allow to drain and dry.

The second way to remove the contents of the egg is preferred in some instances because it can be done by piercing only one hole in the egg. Also, if you are planning on decorating a great many eggs, this way is easier and more efficient.

Purchase a piece of rubber tubing, about ¼-inch in diameter and with a ⅛-inch hole, about 16 inches long (automotive supply stores usually carry this tubing). Now, take an empty ball-point pen; remove and wash the small plastic tube which held the ink. With a knife slice off one end just a tiny bit to form a point. Insert the blunt end of the plastic tube into the end of the rubber tube just deeply enough to hold firmly; about ½-inch should do this. This will leave about 1½ inches of the plastic tube extending from the rubber tube. This should be at the pointed end.

Now, take the egg and pierce a hole in one end with a small nail or pin, making it large enough to insert the tube with a small area of open shell around it so that the contents will have space to emerge. Hold the egg upright with the hole at the bottom and the tube inserted over a bowl and blow gently into the other end of the tube. This is a very easy way to work and will not require the hard blowing sometimes necessary to remove the contents by the two-hole method.

After the eggs are blown out, you dye the shells in the same manner as described before.

With the eggs colored and the contents removed we are now ready to decorate the eggs with the preserved flowers.

First of all, plan your color design for contrast and form. The preserved flowers will still retain a surprising amount of their original color; pansies, daisies, and roses, especially, look almost as they did when growing in the garden.

A good color contrast is pink rose petals on a blue egg, or deep red rose petals on a yellow egg. Do not try to arrange your flowers as they are found in nature. What we are working toward is flat, or nearly flat, flower and petal arrangements on the eggs, and to achieve this you will have to use single petals of such flowers as roses, zinnias, and marigolds. Tansy leaves, ferns, and small weeds and grasses may be used wherever desirable for an artistic effect. I like to draw the fine stems and tendrils on later, after the petals have been placed on the eggs. For this I use a fine pen and India ink in several colors, principally black, brown, and green.

For the actual glueing of the flower petals on the eggs I prefer to use clear or transparent jewelry cement, brushing the glue on the eggshell just on the area where I plan to place the petal.

Pick up the petal either with your fingers, a pair of tweezers, or a moistened Q-tip. With a soft cloth, just barely dampened in water, pat the flower petal in place with a gently rolling motion, making certain the petals are smoothly affixed to the shell and any excess glue is removed.

I find it most practical to work on only one side of an egg at a time, taking up another to decorate while the first one is drying. With an assortment of preserved flowers on hand, you will have plenty of material to choose from and can probably decorate five or six eggs at a time, taking each one up in turn.

Place the decorated eggs in an empty egg carton for easy storage. I usually cut off the tops of the cartons so nothing will mar the tops of the eggs should the glue on the end flower, which closes the hole, be a bit sticky.

Letting the flower petals dry completely on the eggs is something I never like to hurry. In my opinion, a week is not too long, but the final finish can be put on sooner if time is of the essence and you have a deadline to meet.

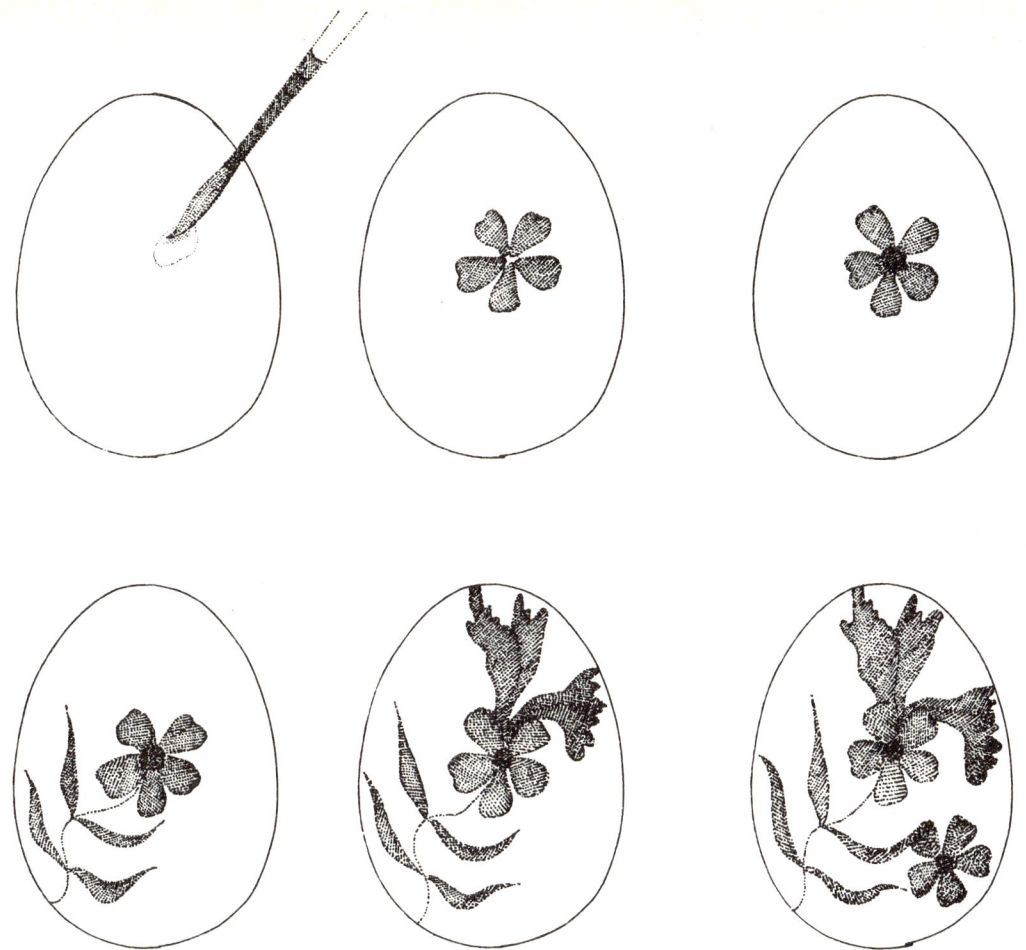

Gluing petals: Brush glue on shell only where petal is to be placed. Pat petals and leaves in place gently with damp cloth, one by one until flower is formed. Allow to dry after each placement.

Here is my big surprise for the finishing touch. Have you ever seen the sunlight glint on the sides of a live minnow? That's just exactly the effect you will get with Pearl Lacquer (Herter's Pearl Lacquer, available from Herter's, Inc., Rural Route 1, Waseca, Minnesota 56093). This lacquer gives a beautiful pearl finish while retaining the original color underneath it.

If you have decorated some white eggs and want to give them additional color, you can add a drop of Herter's Celluloid Enamel to the white pearl. This enamel comes in yellow, orange, red, black, green, blue, and purple.

If you want an extra pearly effect you can use two coats of this lacquer. Allow it to dry for several hours, or overnight, between coats. If you have a buildup from the first coat, sand with very fine sand paper. I find the pearl lacquer is easiest to apply with a flat ¼ to ½

Attaching flower petals to egg.

inch paint brush. If you use this enamel you should also get a bottle of the special thinner for cleaning your brush each time you use it.

If you are wondering how I came by this unusual craft material, I slipped it out of my husband's supply of special paints—the ones he uses for refinishing his artificial baits. There were some other, even more fantastic paints in that box, too. More about these later on.

If you would prefer to finish these eggs in a low-gloss finish, without the pearly look, they may be painted with Hyplar Matte Medium & Varnish. Otherwise the procedure for finishing the eggs is the same as I have outlined.

CHAPTER THREE

Rose-Scented Eggs

Fragrant eggs? Yes, why not? These beautiful, aristocratic eggs please both our senses, sight and smell.

You will need rose petals to make them. My idea for these eggs was inspired by the rose beads that many women used to make here in Oklahoma and Texas in pioneer days. These were very popular in the old days when costume jewelry was not as easily come by as it is now and creative women enjoyed making their own.

Any roses will do, but I particularly like the hybrid perpetuals such as George Dickson or Ulrich Brunner, or the hybrid teas, Etoile de Hollande, and E. G. Hill. If I want to make a lot of rose beads, I turn to my pink dawn climber which is almost a solid wall of shell-pink, fragrant roses that flower so profusely I can pick and pick and the blossoms never thin out.

Picking at the right time of day is important and you will find your most fragrant roses in the sunniest and most protected spot in the garden: it is there that they develop their essential oils to the highest degree. Collect the flowers early in the morning before the sun is high on a dry day after two or three days of dry weather.

For this purpose, never use rain-soaked flowers or those that have been open for several days and are about to shatter. Also, fragrant oils will not be present in the already cut flowers that you may have been using to decorate the house. For rose beads, fresh, just-opening roses are a must.

After picking a basketful of petals, being careful to pull petals only—no leaves, stems or centers are ever used—I put them through my kitchen food chopper. The chopper must be well scrubbed in advance and thoroughly dried in the warm sun so that no trace of odor from food clings to it. This is a delicate business and we should be careful not to mix aromas.

Color of petals is of no consequence because once they are ground they will all turn a dark, rich brown no matter what their original color was.

When you grind the petals, place a receptacle underneath the chopper; they usually contain more moisture than apparent, and this will drop out in the grinding process.

After the petals are ground, place them in a deep bowl and add olive oil a few drops at a time, stirring and pressing it into the petal mixture. Test as you go along so that you will not add too much. It should be of just the right consistency to be shaped into small balls in the palm of your hand.

The instructions for rose beads, which I got from an old newspaper clipping published around 1902, are to pat out the mixture on a piece of wax paper to a thickness of about ½-inch. The charming directions continue by saying "cut each bead-to-be with an old-fashioned gold wedding band"—just as you would a batch of biscuits or ginger cookies! After being cut, the beads are shaped into round balls and pressed on hatpins. The beads are then laid on a sheet of wax paper to dry. Though they seem large they will shrink to about two-thirds or even half their size when completely dry, which takes about a month.

The beads, which become very dark after drying, contrast well with brilliants and pearls. Their principal function was to add fragrance which will last for years if the beads have been correctly made. The odor is especially noticeable in a closed room.

For the beads I use for decorating the eggs, I follow exactly the same procedure but make the beads much, much smaller, tailoring them in size depending on whether I will use them to decorate goose, duck, or chicken eggs. Because these beads are so much smaller, they will dry more quickly than those intended for the necklace and, since I do not plan to thread them on a string, I do not put them on pins of any sort.

I like to plan the design of these rose-scented eggs around a small, 13- × 18-mm. jewelry stone of the type used in pendants and pins. These are to be found in a number of exquisite colors and designs in the

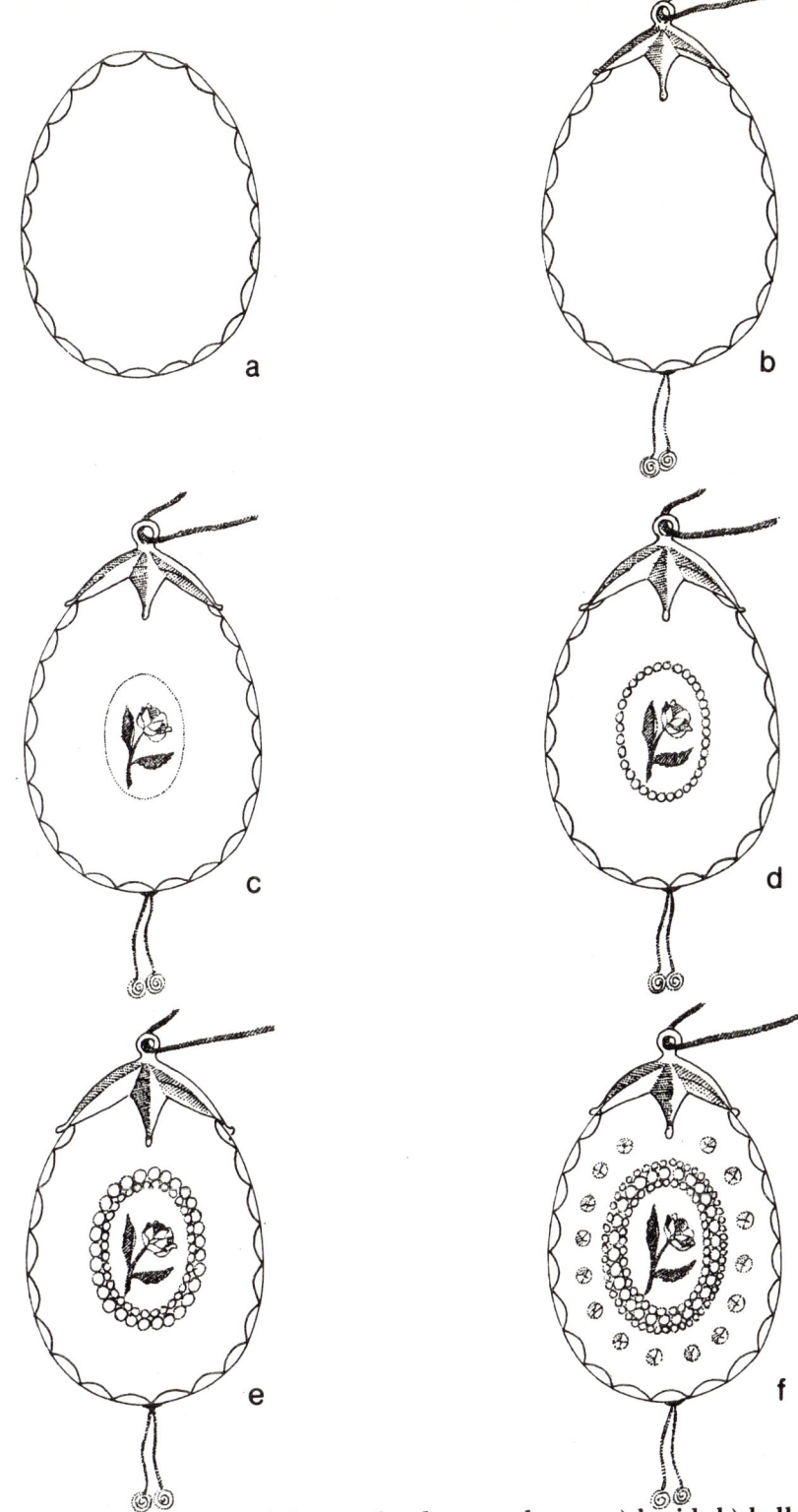

Making Rose Bead eggs: Materials are glued on as shown; a) braid; b) bell cap (attach rose beads); c) jewelry stone; d) pearls; e) rose beads; f) another circle of pearls; rhinestones.

Rose-scented eggs, displayed on an antique lamp.

catalog of Grieger's, Inc., 1633 East Walnut Street, Pasadena, California 91109.

For a large goose egg decorated in this manner, you might prefer a larger stone; if so, they, too, are available. I chose most of my stones from the Rosa Grande collection in blue and rose, but I also ordered some of the 17 × 16 mm. stones from the "Delicate Hearts" collection.

Other delightful possibilities are tea rose, antique rose, dusty rose, and pink, and the lovely golden rose and silver rose stones. The latter may be obtained on a background of green, red, white, or black, and are simply stunning when used on these eggs. Other possibilities are tiny oval stones of French court ladies and gentlemen with roses in their hands—these will give your rose eggs a lovely antique touch and make them seem even more precious.

Something else I have on hand is a supply of gold and silver color rose beads which can usually be purchased at a craft shop. I use two of these, threaded on gold or silver thread, and attach them to the bottom of the egg when it is hung. Bell caps and tiny braid or ribbon for hangers should also be ready.

For the "silver" egg, I start by blowing out the contents of the egg by either of the two methods previously described. After the egg is cleaned and completely dry I paint it all over with silver color "liquid leaf," allowing this to dry.

Then I center the oval blue rose jewelry stone, glue it with contact glue, and surround it with a frame of white 2-mm. pearls. Next, I frame the pearls with the dried rose beads which are, in turn, framed by another row of white pearls. These pearls will go on easily and neatly if strung on thread and curved around the jewelry stone and rose beads. Make a circle of glue (transparent jewelry cement is best for this) and lay the threaded beads around the stone on the glue, cutting your thread just where the beads come together to make an exact fit.

When this part of your project has dried completely (and I always stress allowing everything to dry well before continuing, otherwise your fingers may stick and pull your work out of place; I know this can be very discouraging because it has happened to me several times when I was hurrying to finish something—make haste slowly), dot the clear cement around and about 1/4-inch away from the last row of pearls for the rhinestone trim. For the silver-painted egg, I used blue rhinestones to harmonize with the blue-rose jewelry stone. If you want particularly well crafted rhinestones you will be able to obtain these also from Grieger's in many sizes and almost every imaginable color.

To finish the egg I run a strip of silver braid around it from top to bottom to top, affixing the bell cap at the top with contact glue and sewing rose beads to the braid at the bottom.

The gold-colored egg was completed in exactly the same design using pearls, rose beads, and garnet-colored rhinestones.

The copper egg was tinted with Festique Spangle Copper which I obtained at a ceramic supply house. It is made by Africana, 2079 State Road 131, Batavia, Ohio. This is a paste, applied with your fingers, and should be buffed lightly when completely dry. I used a strip of copper braid, obtained at a fabric center, to complete this, in addition to rhinestones in shades of brown and golden topaz, arranged around and 1/4-inch from the last row of pearls.

The white egg was painted with two coats of Herter's Pearl Lacquer. The rose jewelry stone was surrounded by pearls, then the rose beads (as with the others), but to give greater contrast I used gold beading for the final row. The rest of the egg area was completely covered with pearl cup sequins.

If you want to make these eggs in quantity I would suggest painting several at a time in silver, gold, copper, and pearl. This will reduce the chore of brush cleaning and make your paint go further. If you want something for a special and most unusual gift you will find these rose eggs are greatly cherished by anyone fortunate enough to be a recipient.

CHAPTER FOUR

Jeweled Eggs for All Occasions

Another delightful custom that has come to us from several European countries is the egg tree. The hollow decorated shells are suspended from one branch, several branches grouped together in a vase, or a small tree. This tree can be of any type with branches evenly spaced, or interestingly twisted—you can even use driftwood.

Here in the Southwest where I live, manzanita and mesquite are easily obtainable, or I may use dogwood or redbud branches. If you cannot get out into the country to find a tree or branches, Lee Wards (Elgin, Illinois, 60120) features a very attractive brass ornament hanger in their fall and winter catalog. This hanger has wire "arms" which can be moved to various positions to give the best display effect and the hanger itself may be suspended from a light fixture or doorway—wherever you wish to display your decorated eggs to the greatest advantage.

If you do find a small tree or branch to your liking, it will make a more effective background if it is sprayed or painted white, gold, or silver (or another color if you are trying for a definite color scheme). I used two coats of white acrylic house paint, which doesn't turn yellow, for my tree. Liquid leaf in gold or silver looks well for a metallic effect.

Before you paint the tree, wrap the branches here and there with small, thin wire to make additional egg hangers; this insures that they will be evenly spaced when they are on the tree. Paint these wires when you do the tree and they will not be noticeable.

Set your little tree firmly in a small flower pot. Place a piece of cardboard over the draining hole in the pot, put the tree upright, and fill the ground around it with rocks, gravel, or coarse sand. You may then paint the pot to match the tree or cover it with crepe or metallic paper, finishing with a bow or braid or a ruffle of wide lace.

For this tree I used all white eggshells, emptied by the blowing method previously described. All were colored, using Maid of Scandinavia Cakolor, in many different shades.

After the eggs have been blown out, colored, and dried, I band each one with a strip of braid. This may be black and gold, white and gold, or pastel shades of pink, blue, violet, and yellow which are especially pretty for Easter eggs when lighter colors seem more appropriate.

Odd as it may seem, no egg is exactly like any other egg—they are as individually different as fingerprints, no matter how much they may look alike. So, when you cut your braid, measure it each time around the egg you intend to use it on, and cut the strip just long enough to fit the egg lengthwise. Do not let it overlap at the end or you will have a bunch effect and it will be more difficult to put the bell cap over it. If you cannot get an exact fit it is better to have a tiny gap.

When you have measured the braid, cut it and lay it aside. Now dot white glue around the egg and place your strip of braid over the glue, pressing down firmly. Hold it in place for a few minutes, until it begins to set and then place it upright back in the egg carton to dry completely.

While the first egg is drying, I like to take up another egg and repeat the same operation, using a different color braid or one of the metallic braids. Again I measure the egg to allow for any fractional differences in size, cut, glue, and place.

By the time I am ready for the next step, the first egg is nicely dry. I like to put the braid on first because it makes all the other steps so much easier if I have something firm to hold the egg with.

And now the bell cap which will go at the top of the egg. You may want to make a hanger for this from braid, thin wire, silk or velvet ribbon. Or perhaps you may have some small broken chains of gold or silver in your jewelry box that will do nicely and add to the jewelry effect of the eggs. Whatever you decide to use, attach it firmly to the bell cap before you glue it on to the egg.

Glue the bell cap on to the end of the egg where the braid has terminated so any space will be neatly covered. Use either clear jewelry cement or contact glue as either of these will hold better than white glue.

An ornament at the bottom of the egg adds length, grace, and

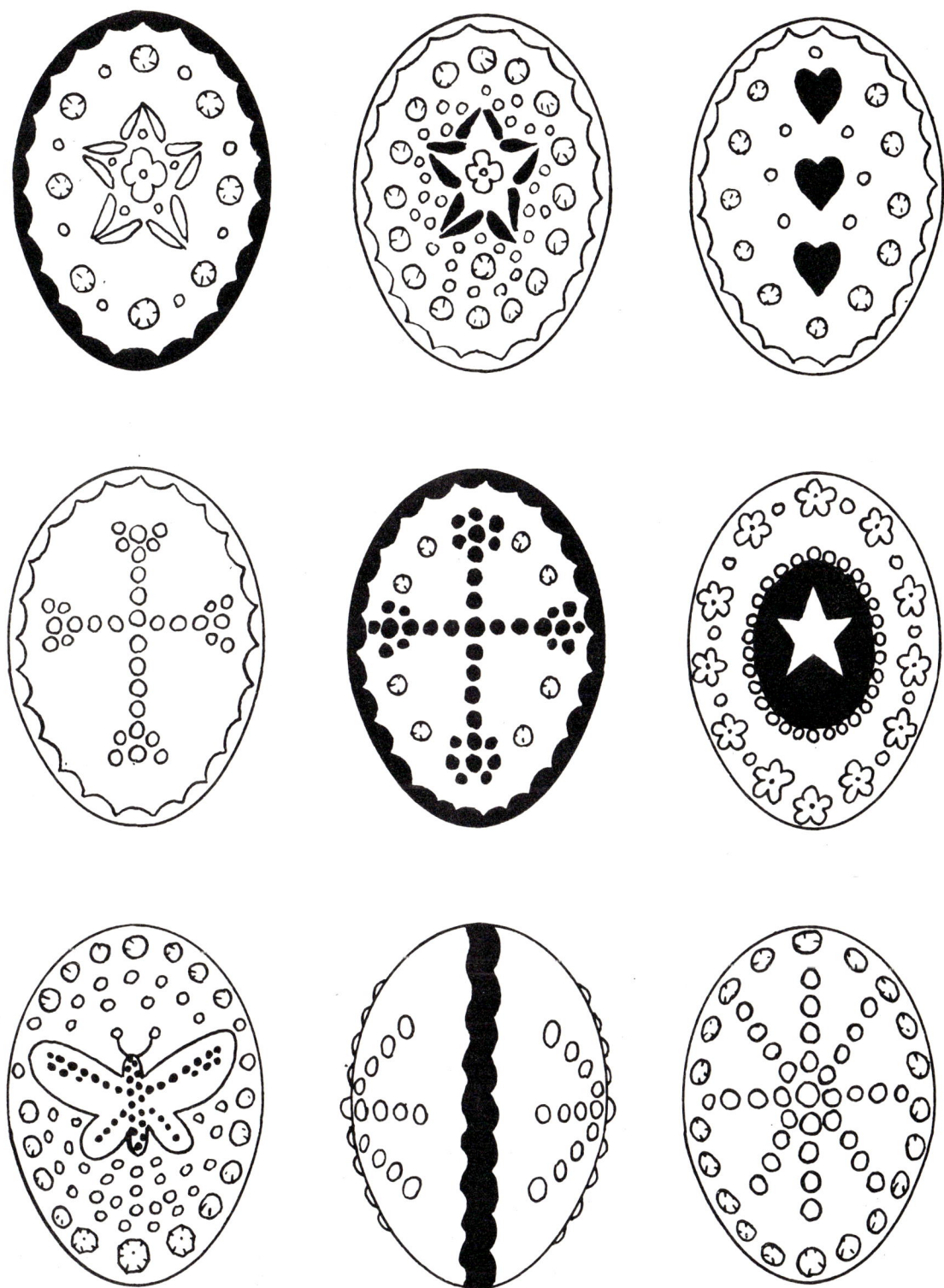

Suggestions for different designs using braid, sequins and beads as decoration.

additional interest. I will describe these individually as I give directions for each egg.

If these eggs are to be used as an Easter decoration we will be using designs for many of them that have religious meaning. Some symbols, such as the cross and the butterfly, are used at both Christmas and Easter—others are particular to each season and should be considered separately.

There is the interesting legend of the little Castilian donkey, or ass, which is a symbol of Easter because of a dark line of hair running the length of his back, crossed by another one over his shoulders. The reason for this, so the story goes, is because the ass was the animal Christ chose to ride on during his triumphal entry into the city of Jerusalem.

The Phoenix, also a symbol of the Resurrection, is used because it is supposed to rise from its own ashes to live again, signifying that one can die and be born anew.

Strangely enough the lion (I found one in a tiny silk shield at a fabric center, just the right size to fit on an egg) is also an Easter symbol, and for a very odd reason. Ancient people believed that lion cubs were born dead. It was thought that after the cubs were three days old the lioness breathed on them and thus brought them to life. Because of this curious belief, the lion became an Easter symbol, signifying the fact that Christ lived again after lying three days in the tomb.

The legend of the eagle is closely related to that of the phoenix because in ancient times it was thought that the eagle restored its life by flying so close to the sun that its feathers were scorched and burned. Still burning, the eagle would plunge downward into water and its plumage would be miraculously restored.

Other birds, such as the swallow, have legends woven about them also. Supposedly on the day of the Crucifixion, a swallow flew near the cross on Calvary. According to an old Scandinavian legend, he felt very sorry for Jesus and wished to help Him. He called out "Svale! Svale!" which means "Cheer up! Cheer up!" From that time on the swallow became known as the "Bird of Consolation" or "Swallow." Also, it was thought that, since the swallow wasn't seen all winter, he hibernated in the mud. They believed that he came out in the springtime and this, too, was considered a new birth or Resurrection.

Bells are an Easter symbol because there was a story that they flew to Rome on Maundy Thursday and returned on the Saturday before Easter dropping eggs for the children along the way; also, because they peal out the joyful Easter music.

Palms are very definitely a symbol of Easter and, in Mexico, the Palm

Sunday procession is like a walking garden. All children, accompanied by their parents, carry huge bouquets of palm leaves, fragrant flowers, and laurel as they go to church to receive the priest's blessing. The Mexicans will carefully keep the plants that have been blessed until the next year, for they believe that by so doing they will be protected from sickness.

The women of Mexico and Puerto Rico, and other Latin American countries, also weave the palm leaves into crosses, some large, some very small (tiny enough to decorate an egg), but all must be blessed.

You may wish to place some tiny, flower-trimmed hats on some of your Easter eggs. While these are not in any way a religious symbol, the custom of wearing new clothes on Easter Sunday is so widespread that the "Easter bonnet" has become an Easter symbol to many of us.

Butterflies, also symbols of the Resurrection, are especially bright and pretty when used as decorations for Easter eggs. You may buy them already made of gold paper, or make them yourself. Maid of Scandinavia has some very pretty ones, made of brightly colored plastic, mounted on wire, which are very effective when affixed to the top of an egg. If you have placed your egg hanger in a doorway or some place where it will catch a light breeze, the butterflies will give the effect of having just alighted. Tiny, gossamer, nylon butterflies are also available. These, too, are mounted on wire and have a wingspread of less than an inch. A tiny bit of glitter on their wings adds much to their charm.

Many plants are Easter symbols and some can be used to form tiny decorations. The hawthorn tree, from which, according to a Czechoslovakian legend, the crown of thorns worn by Christ was made, is a plant that has taken on Easter significance.

I have in my yard a jujube tree, a species of hawthorn grown for its edible fruits, which has long thorns and I have many times used these for decoration.

The thistle is another Easter symbol. The species preserves well, and I have used them in groups of three as decorations. According to some legends, these were also used in the crown of thorns.

The anemone, which the old masters often portrayed in their pictures of the Crucifixion, is a dainty little flower which is said to have sprung up around the base of the cross. On each one of the petals is a red spot which is supposed to symbolize the blood of Christ.

The dogwood has a particularly beautiful flower which is easy to draw and cut from white felt.

Flowers of all sorts are symbols of Easter, for each one, like trees and plants, represents new birth and new life as it springs upward through the dark earth from a tiny seed.

The first egg I am going to describe requires a tiny sequin flower. It is conventionalized and has eight petals. After putting on a piece of black and gold braid and affixing the hanger (bell cap and braid), I put a sequin ½ inch in diameter in the center of the egg. Since the basic color of the egg was yellow, I chose a contrasting metallic green.

I made a frame of double petal, metallic green sequins around the center, about ¼-inch away, and then placed a band of large cup sequins (also in metallic green) between the petals and the braid.

The egg was finished with a pendant drop made of a large pearl sewn to the braid at the bottom of the egg.

I wrapped a green egg with a strip of pink silk braid with a tiny thread of silver; centered it with a six-pointed sequin star in deep green; surrounded this with white iridescent cup sequins; then placed a row of large, deep green cup sequins next to the braid and finished the egg also with a pearl drop at the bottom.

There are several methods of placing the sequins on the egg which I will describe for you as you may find one way easier than the others. With a soft pencil, make tiny dots where you want to place the sequins so they will be as evenly spaced as possible—after you have made a few eggs you will not need to continue to do this—but for the first two or three it will help you to get the "feel" of this part of the job.

After your design is drawn and planned, take up a toothpick of the flat type and use the small end for dotting white glue on the spots you have marked. After marking four or five dots I usually find there is just enough glue left on the toothpick to enable me to pick up the beads or sequins and place them on the egg. This is the most rapid method of decorating for me and you will find yourself picking up speed as you become more adept.

If you find picking up the sequins with a pair of tweezers easier, you may prefer that method.

Plan to make several eggs at a time. Put your sequins, beads, etc. in a couple of TV dinner trays (or other divided dishes) and they will stay together without mixing. I find it helps me to make quick selections if I keep small figurines stored in clear spice bottles.

Another handy way to store materials is to get one of the small cabinets with removable, plastic see-thru drawers. These also have drop-in dividers, and identification labels which fit each drawer front. I keep my different-colored rhinestones in such a cabinet and find it very convenient. These cabinets can be purchased (Sears, Roebuck & Co., or your local hardware store) in several different sizes, from 18 to 48 inches.

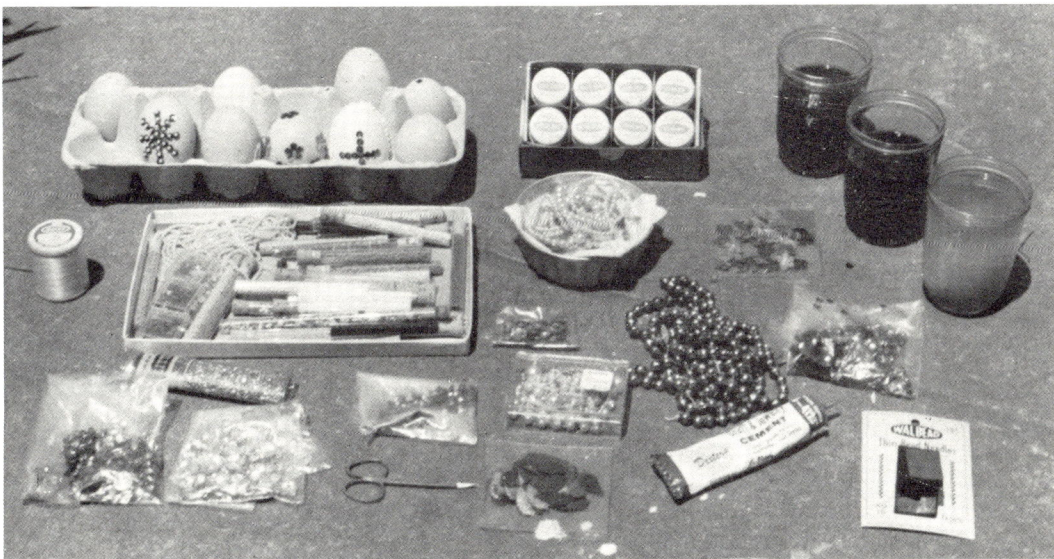

Placing sequins on eggs using toothpicks (top). Necessary equipment should be readily available before you start (bottom).

As you work, you will find that you can make better progress if you plan each design in advance so you will know exactly what color beads or sequins you will want to use. Take them out and have them ready before you start.

Pick up each egg in turn, dot on the glue and place a few sequins. Place this one down to dry, and take up another one and repeat. This works well for me even on those days when I am most fumble-fingered, because most of the hazards of egg decoration seem to occur when a decoration is pushed or slipped out of place before it has completely dried.

Sometimes the use of harmonizing sequins in two different colors, or two shades of the same color, will be lovely. One of my prettiest egg designs features three tiny silver sequin hearts centered on the egg in a vertical pattern. These are surrounded by white seed beads, which are banded by white iridescent sequins surrounded by dark blue sequins, which are, in turn, banded by cerise sequins. In each of the sequins, after it dried, I placed a pink seed bead in the center to cover the tiny hole. A pink pearl was placed in the center of each silver heart.

This egg has a band of black and gold braid run around it lengthwise, a gold bell cap with a gold rickrack hanger, and the pendant at the bottom is a one loop oval cage (Lee Wards), into which I pressed an 8 mm. pearl. Tiny $3/8$-inch marbles in various colors will also fit into these cages.

Marbles for these cages can be made more attractive by giving them a crackle finish. To do this, place clear glass marbles of the correct size and various colors into a pan in your oven. Heat the marbles thoroughly in a fairly high oven and, upon removing them, drop them carefully into cold water.

Larger marbles, treated in this manner, may also be glued to bell caps or used as pendants when sewn to the bottom of the eggs. You can even lengthen this further by placing another bell cap on the end of the marble and put a still smaller marble or pearl into another bell cap, joining the two together with a tiny bit of wire or needle and thread.

Marbles do not have to be of any special type; those you find at the dime store will work just fine.

Pink, white, and gold is another precious color combination. I started with an egg colored a deep shade of shell pink, banded it with white and gold braid, affixed the bell cap and a caged pearl for the drop ornament. I drew a small Latin cross on the egg and filled in the outline with tiny pearls. I left the area around the cross undecorated so the pink background would emphasize the pearls, but I did run a row of white, iridescent sequins around the edge of the braid.

I chose a blue egg to decorate next, banding it with a strip of all-white braid. For the central decoration I cut a small, round piece of black velvet, approximately one inch in diameter. After glueing this down, I placed a five-point sequin star in the center of the velvet. I covered the rough edge of the velvet with white sequins. I placed silver, six-petal flower sequins around the edge of the white braid, then filled in the open space between the flower sequins and the white sequins with silver cup sequins.

A yellow egg was made in a very similar manner by using deep blue sequins very effectively.

Don't overlook the decorative possibilities of buttons and jewelry stone cameos. The button I used for decorating a rose-colored egg was black with the "cameo" in white. The jewelry stone, used for decorating an egg of deeper rose, was ordered from Griegers. It is listed as "Fabulous Cameo" and is a crystal on black, mirrorlike hematite. The size I ordered was 13 × 18 mm. Both button and cameo jewelry stone were surrounded by a row of tiny pearls glued with jewelry cement.

One of the things I commonly find around my garden are tiny, cast-off snail shells, averaging slightly larger than 1/4-inch in diameter. One day I gathered a number of these of uniform size and decided to see what I could do with them. I was intrigued by their small size and graceful shape. I began by washing them in soap suds, rinsing carefully and laying them out to dry in the sun on a piece of absorbent paper toweling.

After they were thoroughly dry, I painted half of them in Liquid Gold and the other half in Liquid Leaf Silver. The silver shells I glued on the surface of a blue egg and surrounded them with five or six silver sequins each. When the silver sequins were dry, I put a deep blue bead in each tiny cup. This egg was pure enchantment so I went to work with the gold shells next.

I dotted these in the same manner all around a deep purple egg, surrounding them with pale violet cup sequins into each of which I dotted a white seed bead.

Both of these eggs were finished at the bottom with 3/4-inch gold filigree cones.

Two of my jeweled eggs were decorated with butterfly sequins for the central design. For the first, a pink egg, I placed the green sequin butterfly in the center, surrounded it with silver cup sequins, then added a band of large, deep green sequins of the same shade as the butterfly. The braid used on this egg was pink and silver and the drop ornament a large pearl.

The second butterfly egg was banded with gold and white braid on a light green egg. I centered the butterfly which was also of metallic green and surrounded it with silver sequins. Then I filled out the space between the silver sequins and braid with three rows of green sequins.

A bright, quick, and easy way to cover a great many eggs effectively, if quantities are needed for a large tree or other decoration, is to completely cover the eggs in a random pattern of two colors of sequins. For one such egg I used red and deep blue on a pink background. Another was brightly decorated in violet and yellow—still another light blue and pink. White, gold, or silver will combine attractively with all colors. There are almost limitless combinations which can also be varied by the base color of the egg itself.

One of my hobbies is rock hounding, particularly surface mining for semiprecious stones. Over the years I have accumulated quite a collection of small, flawed stones. These are not valuable enough to be cut into jewels, but I consider them just right for really unusual egg decorations.

Iridescent fire opal from Mexico, glowing with a ruby orange flame, looks marvelous on a deep violet egg, for the tiny stones are just as brilliant as the larger ones and as the egg is turned from side to side the rainbow fire is just as apparent.

Another exquisite color combination using fire opals starts with a turquoise-blue egg. Using tiny gold rickrack braid, I divided this into four sections, vertically. In the center of each section, using jewelry cement, I glued a small piece of fire opal. I surrounded the fire opal with a band of pearls, and the pearls with iridescent white sequins. Other than attaching a bell cap and hanger at the top and a gold filigree cone at the bottom I did not put on any more decoration—nor did the egg need any.

In southern Oklahoma, where I live, we find agatized wood on the beaches of Lake Texoma, on the border between Oklahoma and Texas, and also tiny, softly rounded stones of white and rose quartz. These last, combined on a turquoise or lemon-yellow egg, look like something out of fairyland touched with a wisp of magic.

Other mineral formations peculiar to our state are the strange barites called "rose" stones. Many of these rosy pink stones actually have petals resembling a rose—and some are small enough to be used as a decoration on an egg. Some of these I have left in their natural color, others I have painted gold or silver. I never use more than two of these to an egg—they look best on a large goose or duck egg—as they are a little heavy, but attractively framed in beads and sequins they can be most handsome.

Sequin-decorated eggs dress up a converted hat stand.

Another stone I find interesting for occasional use are the tiny crinoids found in my area. These little stones, looking for all the world like "cheerios" are real fossils and originated millions of years ago when this part of the world was an inland sea. They were a transitional form between plant and animal life. They are scattered here over a wide area and the tiny ones glue easily to eggs.

Do not put on too many—if you are able to find these or buy them from a store which deals in rocks and fossils—just dot them here and there on an egg that you have painted in gold, silver, or copper. When they are firmly affixed and dry, take a very fine camel-hair brush and color each one individually, being careful not to get paint on the egg. I like to do each little circle a different color. These eggs are a real conversation piece and it's a lot of fun to have your answer ready when people ask what they are. (For painting these you can use acrylic, enamel, or oil paint.)

Something else we are lucky to have in Oklahoma are fresh water pearls. These are real pearls and are found in Oklahoma lakes. They have sheen and luster, some are pink and some are white, but they are usually irregular in shape. I saved some as a memento from a particularly pleasant summer holiday and they turned out to be just the right thing for a pretty egg decoration.

A combination of the eggs decorated with fresh water pearls (or pearl beads) and the ones decorated with shells makes a lovely centerpiece for your table, especially if it is placed on a round mirror for a lovely underwater effect and a few wisps of cured seaweed added here and there.

Every state has semiprecious stones that you can find no matter where you live, and precious stones, too. Diamonds of significant size have been found in reasonable quantities in at least 15 counties in Georgia and other states as well as the famous diamond mines in Arkansas.

To learn more about the goodies in your own state, write for the Geological Survey Bulletin 1042-G, "Gem Stones of the United States," which may be obtained from the Superintendent of Documents, United States Government Printing Office, Washington, D.C. 20402 (price: 35 cents). This will tell you by state and locality where to look and what variety of stones you will find. And you might get a good book on gems from your local library and bone up a little on how to recognize the stones you are most apt to find.

Most of the other materials which have been used for the jeweled eggs, such as braid, ribbon, beads and sequins, were purchased from craft shops, boutiques, or stores that sell yard goods. The local five-and-dime store, even the discount houses are good places to look for "findings." Ask your friends for broken costume jewelry, chains and pendants all of which make interesting decorations. If you have only one really good stone, center it to make it look more important and surround it with beads and sequins.

In the fall save seeds of unusual shapes as these can be lacquered and used with distinction. If you live in a city apartment and cannot get out into the country to look for seeds, consider the possibilities of rice, barley, and small beans. Even small spaghetti, pasta dots, and square pasta present an opportunity often overlooked for a decorative medium right from your own kitchen.

And don't forget tiny candies. If you cannot find the gold and silver decorating balls at your local supermarket, you can get them from Maid of Scandinavia. They may be purchased here in several different sizes and also in colors of pink, blue, and green.

If you are decorating hard-cooked eggs for children, you might like to know about the harlequin trims. These (also obtainable from Maid of Scandinavia) are completely edible and come in several gay colors and shapes. There are red hearts, tiny blossoms, and poker and bridge designs in pastel colors.

Other edible possibilities are tiny icing flowers of calla lilies, daffodils, tulips, hyacinth, pansies and roses.

There are Halloween, Thanksgiving and Christmas assortments, very tiny and all edible. There are even tiny icing rabbits in assorted colors of blue, pink, green, yellow, and orchid, just $1^{1}/_{8}$ inches high. There are clowns, chubby chicks and tiny doves, bluebirds and lovebirds. Children would love eggs decorated with these pure sugar candies and you wouldn't need to worry if they ate them!

CHAPTER FIVE

Jeweled Eggs of the Zodiac

Perhaps this chapter is best begun with a quotation from the cosmic doctrine of the Greek sage, Orpheus: "God, the uncreated and incomprehensible Being, created all things; the ether proceeded from him, from this the unshapely chaos and the dark night arose, which at first covered all things. The unshapen mass was formed into the shape of an egg, from which all things have proceeded."

The entire universe has the shape of an egg and everything in it strives to attain the same form, according to this theory of the ancients.

I have long been a student of astrology which is the study of the sun, moon, planets and stars, in an attempt to foretell future events on earth. Essentially, this study is based on the belief that the affairs of men are controlled by the movements and positions of the heavenly bodies.

Whether we believe in astrology or not is, of course, a personal matter, but its signs and symbols are beautiful. Used as decorations, a set of these twelve signs of the Zodiac can make an extremely interesting display.

The eggs I have used are whole, blown, drained, and each colored in different shade of violet, rose, lemon yellow, emerald, turquoise, or red. They would also be striking if made up in a set of twelve using only black, white and gold.

After the eggs were colored and prepared I treated each one in the same way, running a strip of black and gold rickrack braid around each egg and affixing a pearl drop at the bottom.

For the hanger at the top I used narrow gold braid affixed to a gold filigree cap, larger and more ornate than the bell caps used on the jeweled eggs.

Then I cut a small piece of deep black velveteen in a teardrop shape and glued it to the egg with the largest part at the top and the point at the bottom.

To derive the most enjoyment from making a set of these Zodiac eggs I feel it is essential to have an understanding of the signs and know something of their meaning.

In astronomy, the ecliptic is the hypothetical great circle describing the orbit of the earth around the sun, or the apparent path of the sun, during the year. It is divided into twelve equal, alternating positive and negative fields of 30 degrees each, traditionally called "signs of the zodiac."

The moon traverses the twelve fields of the ecliptic during its monthly orbit around the earth and its position at a given time can be readily derived from published tables.

The "signs" used for these eggs are all in gold, exquisitely detailed, and of exactly the right size and proportions to look well on an egg, placed for greater emphasis on a background of black. They may be purchased from the Thieves Market, 118 A St., N.W., Ardmore, Oklahoma 73401. Here, also, you may purchase the filigree caps which I attached to a very tiny hanger and then affixed to the egg with jewelry cement.

For the first sign, Aquarius, the Waterman (January 20 to February 19), I used an egg colored deep purple. The space between the pearls and the braid and the back of the egg was filled in with gold cup sequins. Aquarius is considered to be airy, dry, barren, and masculine. The ruling planet of Aquarius is Uranus, the keyword forward, the tendency toward progress, the lucky day, Sunday, the lucky number, four. The friends of Aquarius are: Aries, Sagittarius, Libra and Gemini (Aquarius, the Progressive).

For the next sign, Pisces, the Fish (February 9 to March 21) I used a lemon-yellow background for the egg and emerald green sequins placed in rows beginning at the edge of the white pearls (Pisces, the Diplomat). Pisces is considered to be watery, fruitful and feminine. The ruling plant is Neptune, the keyword sympathy, the tendency toward idealism, the lucky day, Monday, the lucky number, seven. The friends of Pisces are Cancer, Scorpio, Taurus and Capricorn.

Aries, the Ram, was placed against a turquoise-blue background, filled in with silver cup sequins (March 21 to April 20th). Aries is believed to be fiery, dry, barren, and masculine. Its natives have the pioneering spirit. The ruling planet is Pluto (Mars), the keyword action, the tendency toward impulsiveness, the lucky day, Tuesday, the lucky number, nine. Friends of Aries are Gemini, Leo, Sagittarius, and Aquarius.

Taurus, the Bull (the Reactor), was put on a violet background, filled in with white cup sequins. In the center of each cup I also placed a white iridescent bead (April 20 to May 21). Taurus is considered to be earthy, moist, feminine, and productive. The ruling plant is Venus, the keyword stability, the tendency toward persistence, the lucky day Friday, the lucky number, six. Friends of Taurus are Cancer, Virgo, Capricorn and Pisces.

I put Gemini, the Twins (the Communicator), on a rose-pink egg filled in with sequins in brilliant cerise (May 21 to June 21). Gemini is considered to be airy, dry, barren and masculine. The ruling planet is Mercury, the keyword versatility, the tendency toward diffusion, the lucky day, Wednesday, the lucky number, five. Friends of Gemini are Aries, Leo, Libra and Aquarius.

Cancer, the Crab (the Introvert—June 21 to July 23) is watery, very fruitful and feminine. This egg was carried out in a color scheme of light blue with pink cup sequins; in the center of each sequin was placed a pink iridescent bead. The ruling planet of Cancer is the Moon, the keyword tenacity, the tendency toward patriotism, the lucky day, Monday, the lucky number, two. Friends of Cancer are Virgo, Scorpio, Pisces, Taurus, and Leo.

Leo, the Lion (the Extrovert—July 23 to August 23) is fiery, barren, dry, and masculine. The "Leo egg" is light yellow with rose-pink cup sequins. The ruling planet of Leo is the Sun, the keyword, power, the tendency toward leadership, the lucky day, Sunday, the lucky number, one. Friends of Leo are Aries, Libra, Gemini and Sagittarius.

Virgo, the Virgin (the Server—August 23 to September 22). The Virgo sign is placed on a light violet egg decorated with cerise sequins. The sign of Virgo is considered to be earthy, dry, barren, and feminine. The ruling planet is Mercury, the keyword, discrimination, the tendency toward chastity, the lucky day, Wednesday, the lucky number, five. Friends of Virgo are Taurus, Capricorn Scorpio, and Cancer.

Libra, the Scales (the Harmonizer—September 23 to October 23) happens to be my own sign and I have used a deep turquoise base with light blue iridescent cup sequins for this egg. Libra is considered to be airy, moist, semifruitful and masculine. Libra's ruling planet is Venus, the keyword, balance, the tendency toward justice, the lucky day, Friday, the lucky number, six. Friends of Libra are Aquarius, Leo, Gemini and Sagittarius.

Scorpio, the Scorpion (the Executive—October 23 to November 22). This egg was colored a very light shell pink, the sequins used were iridescent white and I placed a white iridescent bead in each cup. Scorpio is believed to be watery, fruitful and feminine. The ruling planet is Pluto (Mars), the keyword, emotional drive, the tendency toward investigation, the lucky day Tuesday, the lucky number, nine. Friends of Scorpio are Cancer, Virgo, Capricorn, and Pisces.

Sagittarius, the Bowman (the Social Revolutionist—November 22 to December 22). The egg for Sagittarius, sometimes called the Archer, is emerald green, decorated with white cup sequins and white iridescent beads. Sagittarius is considered fiery, dry, barren and masculine. The ruling planet is Jupiter, the keyword, foresight, the tendency toward honesty, the lucky day, Thursday, the lucky number, three. Friends are Aries, Leo, Libra, and Aquarius.

Capricorn, the Goat (the Conservative—December 22 to January 20). This egg base is amethyst with pink cup sequins in the center of which I placed a pink iridescent bead. Capricorn is thought to be earthy, moist, somewhat productive, and feminine. The ruling planet is Saturn, the keyword, ambition, the tendency toward caution, the lucky day, Saturday, the lucky number, eight, and the friends Taurus, Virgo, and Pisces.

Since I made up this set of twelve Zodiac signs for purely decorative purposes, I did not attempt to color the eggs according to the color of the sign. However, for those who would like to have the information I will give the correct color for each sign:

Aquarius: Mingled colors, plaids, changeable hues.
Pisces: All tints of the ocean.
Aries: Red.
Taurus: Blue.
Gemini: Blue and silver gray.
Cancer: Opalescent tints and green.
Leo: Orange.
Virgo: Gray blue.
Libra: Crimson, turquoise, pastel tints.
Scorpio: Green.
Sagittarius: Purple.
Capricorn: Black, dark green, and brown.

If you do not wish to make up an entire set of twelve Zodiac eggs, you might like to make up an egg in the correct sign for each member of your family.

They are equally decorative when placed on stands or hung from a small tree. Displayed like this, they can be placed anywhere and still be

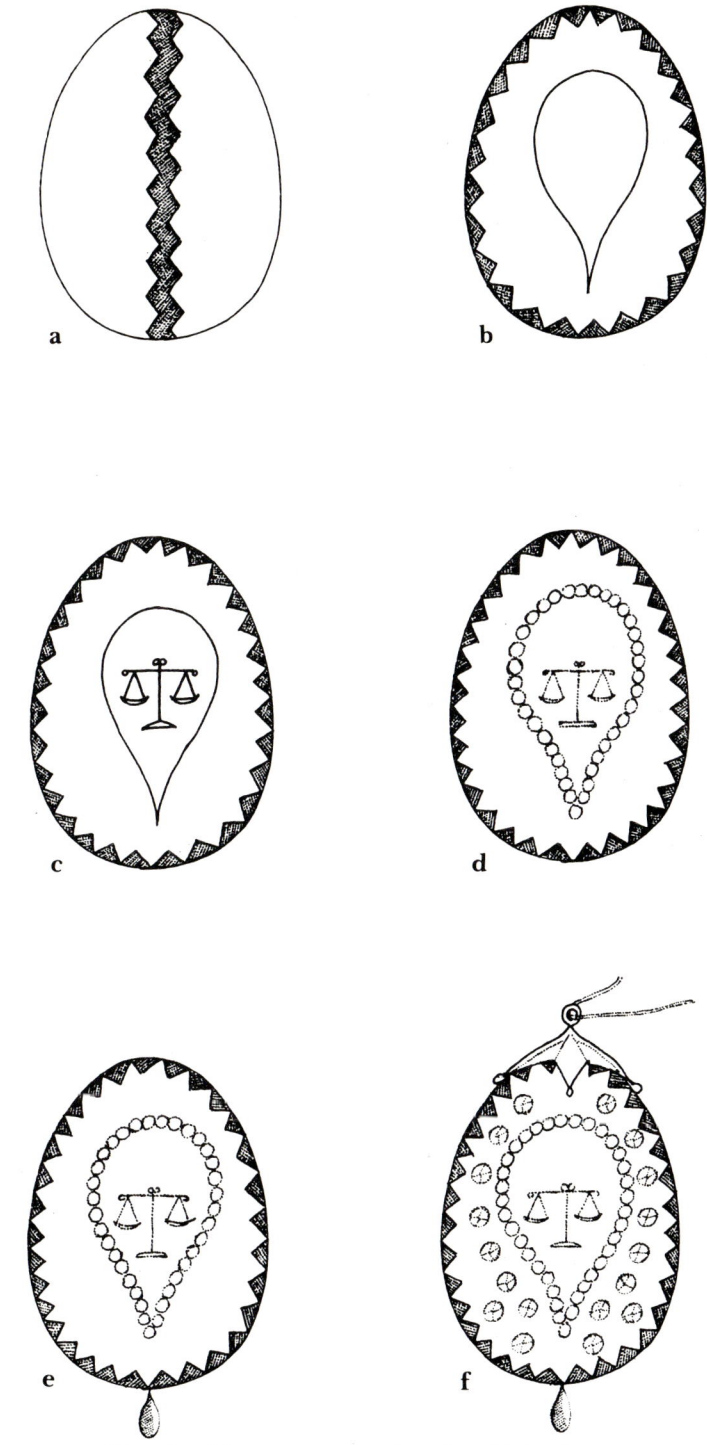

Making Zodiac eggs: a) Glue braid around egg, leaving ⅛-inch gap at top to be covered by bell cap. b) Glue black velvet "teardrop" to center of egg. c) Place tiny gold Zodiac sign on velvet. d) Use tiny pearls to outline velvet teardrop. e) Sew pearl teardrop to braid at bottom of egg. f) Glue bell hanger to top of egg.

a great conversation piece. Later on in this book there is a chapter on how to make your own egg stands. For the Zodiac eggs those that are made to look like antiques are especially appropriate.

Truly, for those who enjoy making decorations that are both sophisticated and currently of great interest, there are few egg designs that are more chic, fun, and fabulous than the Zodiacs.

CHAPTER SIX

Egghead Eggs

Eggheads are so easy to make, so inexpensive, and such fun that even children can participate in this amusing project. The materials required are:

- Blown eggs, white or brown (If you cannot obtain brown eggs for the heads where this color is indicated, dye or paint eggs according to instructions for each character.)
- Fake fur (Try to get small scraps in many different colors.)
- Miniature champagne glasses (Maid of Scandinavia, No. 23639. These are 1¾ inches tall and packed in sets of 12.)
- Curtain rings, approximately 1 inch in diameter (white or gold plastic).
- "Findings" (tiny scraps of velvet, leather or net, beads, paper, rhinestones, etc.).
- Contact glue.

All eggheads are made by first measuring the fake fur hair. Since egg sizes vary so much with seasons and localities, it is possible to give only approximations for the strips of fake fur to be cut. As with the instructions for putting braid around the eggs, you should measure each egg individually. Always be careful to cut the fake fur so that adequate space will be left to clearly draw or paint the features of the face.

Undine, the water nymph, is a particularly easy egghead to begin with. For this I chose a white egg of good shape so the face would be nicely oval. The egg was blown and the interior cleansed, as I explained earlier, and then placed upright in a carton so it would drain thoroughly. (Be careful to do this with all the eggheads.)

When the egg was completely dry I had a strip of light green fake fur ready to put on. This first strip, about 4½ inches long by 1½ inches wide, was for the back part of the head. I put the contact glue on the underside of the fur strip and secured it to the lower part of the egg, leaving a "bald" area at the top.

After the first strip of fur was dry and firmly attached, I cut another strip of the same color fur about 1½ inches long by 1½ inches wide. This I placed where the hair line would normally be on the forehead, pressing it down to cover the bald spot. You need not worry about making this piece fit exactly. When it is dry, take an ordinary hair brush and brush the upper "hair" over and into the lower strip and it will completely cover the spot.

There will be a slightly rough edge showing along the forehead, and this is covered with three tiny pink plastic boutique roses and two green rhinestones, placed alternately. Above the lower row I placed two more roses and one rhinestone. After these were dry I cut tiny leaves (11 in number) and glued these in an arc around the roses and rhinestones.

I would suggest that you practice drawing the features for Undine's face first on another egg, drawing them lightly with a sharp pencil and then outlining them with either a very fine camel-hair brush, using acrylic paint, or a croquill (sometimes spelled crow quill) pen and India ink. The lips are painted with a bit of red mixed with white. The eyes are emerald green.

After the face is painted—and either the acrylic paint or the India ink will dry quickly—secure the lower, pointed end of the egg into one of the gold plastic curtain rings. Let dry.

Now, invert one of the miniature champagne glasses and affix the gold curtain ring to the foot of the glass.

When the ring is firmly set give the "hair" a final brushing and, if you like, you can then spray it with ordinary hair spray to hold it in place.

Undine will make a charming dresser ornament or an unusual party favor. For party favors you can follow this same method, using "hair" of many different shades—there are about 24 shades of fake fur to choose from.

The decorative possibilities of eggheads are limited only by your

The Eggheads: great fun to create.

imagination and they are adaptable to every season of the year. You may affix ribbons or pipe cleaners to them and use them for Christmas tree decorations. A row of them hung in a window will attract everyone's attention. Give them saucy Easter bonnets for the ladies and hats for the gentlemen and hang them from a small decorative tree.

The color of the hair—and the way it is put on—is largely determined by the character you are endeavoring to create.

The Halloween witch, for example, has wild orange hair flying in all directions. This effect was achieved by using three rows of fur, instead of two as I did for Undine. The first row, about one inch in width, was put lower down on the egg—just high enough so it would clear the part of the egg that would be glued to the curtain ring later.

The second row of hair was glued on directly above this and the third scrap of fur placed along the forehead to cover the bald spot as I did for Undine. Then I put a very narrow strip across the forehead and clipped for bangs.

Before I put the fur on this egg I colored its entire surface a light orange, using Cakolor orange (place the egg in a tiny bit, dissolved in warm water, just long enough to tint a pale orange shade). No. 16 from Maid of Scandinavia.

For the eyes, rather heavy eyebrows, and pointed nose I used black acrylic paint, using a fine, No. 1 Grumbacher camel-hair brush. With this same brush I painted a smiling, orange-red mouth and white teeth.

The witch egghead is now ready to be placed in the gold plastic curtain ring and the ring affixed to the foot of the inverted champagne glass. I prefer to put the black velveteen hat on last as it is easier then to set it at a jaunty angle. This rich witch was now dressed in her best coven-go-to-meeting!

I cut both the crown and the brim of the hat from black paper, slashing the center part of the brim into eight points which I folded upward so they would fit into the cone of the crown.

The black paper was covered with deep black velveteen (use velvet, silk or felt, whatever you prefer). The cone was glued to form a tall peak and the points of the brim firmly glued inside the cone. I then cut a narrow strip of black velveteen (you could use ribbon) about 1/4-inch wide, and glued this around the jointure of the crown and brim to produce a neat look.

When the hat was dry I placed glue around the inside of the cone and set the hat on the witch's head, holding it a few minutes so it would adhere without slipping out of place.

Santa Claus: for this the entire egg should be painted or dyed a light shade of rosy pink. Run a strip of white fake fur around the egg for the hair as you did for Undine, at about the same height on the egg. Since Santa wears a cap the top will be left bald.

I found it easier to paint on the features of Santa before applying beard and mustache, so this came next. I gave Santa white, bushy eyebrows outlined with very tiny black pen strokes, using my crow quill pen and India ink.

The bright blue eyes are outlined in black and have black lashes. Cheeks and nose are painted a bright, rosy red, "like a cherry." The smiling mouth is red and slightly open. Between mouth and nose I placed two very tiny pieces of white fake fur, gluing them securely, and when they had dried I looped these upward in a curve (to give a smiling effect), and affixed the end to the hair at the side of the face with a tiny spot of glue.

I cut a piece of white fur about an inch wide and 1 1/4 inches long and glued this to the chin, just below the mouth for Santa's beard.

Make a peaked cap, as you did for the witch, but without the paper to stiffen it, and pull it downward to one side (you can attach a tiny bell if you like).

My first French lady had light violet hair placed on the egg in such a manner that the sweep of the fake fur hair is upward toward the top of her head. A cotton ball was hidden under the hair as it was twisted back and downward and secured with a band of black velvet ribbon. The idea was to have the hairdo resemble the very high coiffures popular with court ladies in the time of Marie Antoinette.

The black velvet band may be given additional decoration in the form of flowers and rhinestones if you wish to make your lady very elegant.

To hide the rough edges of the fur which is drawn upward, I cut very tiny scraps of fur, about ¼-inch wide, and glued them to the back of the head, sweeping the ends toward the face and upward, and securing them with a tiny bit of glue.

The face had delightfully mischievous eyes of deep violet, with the corners slightly slanted upward, long lashes, and curving eyebrows of black acrylic paint.

I mixed a tiny bit of violet and rose with white to get a harmonizing shade for the mouth.

My second French lady had a hairdo of another period. The fake fur hair was a shade which very nearly resembles ash blond. It was glued on with a side part, a small piece drawn around the back of the head, and a larger piece drawn across the forehead. A third piece was set in at the top and this was also drawn down the back and slightly to one side.

Gathering the ends of the three pieces together I concealed the end of a fourth piece. The fourth piece was secured with thread to make it behave, and formed into a large curl which hung downward.

This lady had slanted eyes of emerald green, long black lashes, and and black eyebrows. To further enhance the look of innocence I set the head in a curtain ring of white plastic before gluing it to the champagne glass.

My third lady was of a still later period and she was impish indeed with side-parted auburn hair drawn to the back into a tiny chignon. I rolled this tightly and secured it with contact glue, pressing it down until it held the shape I wanted.

This lady had slanted eyes of emerald green, long black lashes and arched eyebrows. Her tiny nose had piquant freckles. These were dotted on by using the crow quill pen and dark brown India ink. Her open, smiling mouth was rosy red.

My fourth lady could be the little high school girl from down the block. She had brown-blond hair with a side part and a sweet, open expression, large, intelligent blue eyes, and a smiling mouth.

For all four of these ladies I left the eggs completely white. The cheeks could be touched with a very pale pink (white acrylic mixed with a touch of red) if a more made-up look was desired.

The Easter Bunny has always been a very popular fellow and children especially are delighted by the Easter Bunny eggs I give as gifts at Easter time. They make amusing little presents for other folks, too.

All of these eggheads are made with chicken eggs, but I try to choose them carefully for size and shape. I use eggs as large as I can find for the bunnies so the big, floppy ears will be in proportion.

I start by cutting two cardboard (the cardboard that comes from the laundry in your husband's shirts is about the right weight and thickness) ears about $2^{1/4}$ inches long. I clip the bottom $1/4$-inch into three tiny slashes to form little prongs, extending two to the front and one to the back.

Cut two pieces of pink fake fur and glue them to the front of the ears. Do not glue fur on the three little prongs. Let the fur dry for a few minutes and cut two similar size pieces of white to glue to the back of the ears. When the ears are dry, brush the fur together at the edges and spray with hair spray to hold in place.

Glue the ears to the top of the head. The roundness of the egg will just naturally give them the correct outward slant for a jaunty look.

I cut a tiny piece of white fur about an inch long and $1/4$-inch wide and glue this across the forehead in front of the ears to hide the tiny prongs which attach the ears to the head. I clipped the white fur short to make fluffy bangs. A similar piece was glued across the back to cover the prongs.

Two pieces of fur about $1^{1/2}$ inches long and $1/4$-inch wide were glued down on either side of the face and clipped to form fluffs, making a sort of halo around the face.

A piece of fur was glued to the back of the head just below the short piece covering the ear prongs. Measure this before you cut and fit it to the space to be covered. After it is glued and set, it should be clipped short.

As illustrated, the bunny's smiling face is an amusing one and very easy to draw. Blue eyes are placed in comic round circles and a thin line of black eyebrow is arched to follow this shape.

I made a little round dot of a pink nose outlined in black, drew on the mouth and whiskers with black acrylic paint, and gave my bunny two typical large white front teeth which add to his funny expression.

The head was glued to a white plastic curtain ring and the ring glued to the foot of a miniature champagne glass as with the other eggheads.

Who doesn't love a little clown? And this little funny face is one of the easiest of all to make. Start with a white egg, as round as you can find, and beginning at the back of the head, run a piece of red fake fur (about $4^{1/2}$ to 5 inches long and $1/4$-inch wide) all around the face from behind where the ears would be, around the chin, and around to the starting point at the back of the head.

Clip the red fake fur about $1^{1/4}$ inches in front and taper to about one

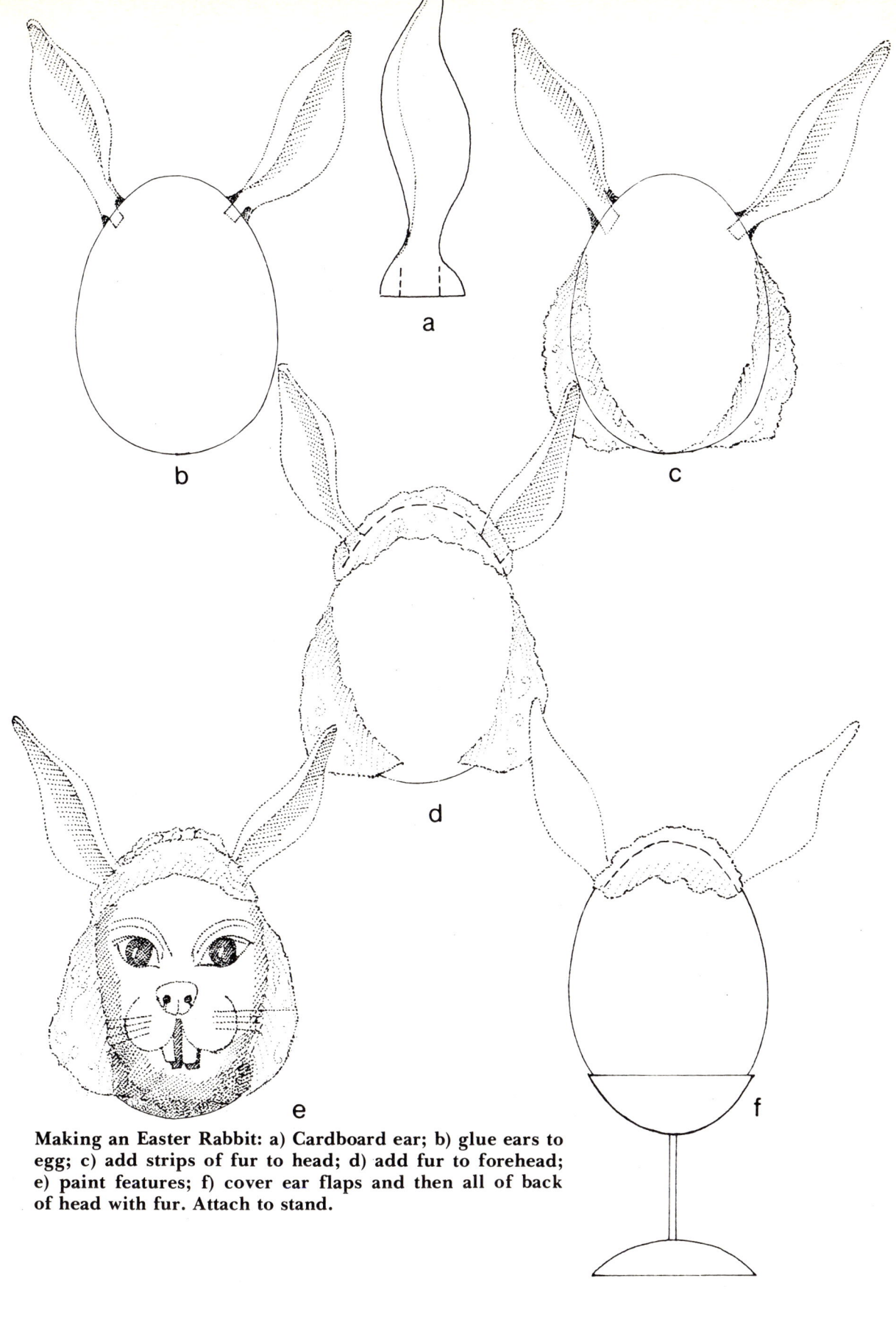

Making an Easter Rabbit: a) Cardboard ear; b) glue ears to egg; c) add strips of fur to head; d) add fur to forehead; e) paint features; f) cover ear flaps and then all of back of head with fur. Attach to stand.

inch as it rounds to the back of the head. Cut and clip a piece about two inches long and ¼-inch wide to form bangs. Leave bald spot at the top of the head.

Form a one-inch-wide piece of blue velveteen into a cone. Twist a tiny scrap of white fur to form a pom-pom at the peak of the cone. Sew blue velveteen together and glue to top of clown's head, covering bald spot.

You are now ready to paint the features on the head. I started by painting a tiny red "spit" curl on the forehead. The eyes are just black triangles and the nose a round red spot. The wide red mouth smiles and the cheeks are just suggested to add to the effect.

Place the clown head on a white plastic curtain ring and glue as with the others.

As you work with the fake fur, more ideas seem to occur for placing it in different ways on the eggs to achieve characterization.

And how about a leprechaun for St. Patrick's Day? This amusing little Irish fairy is usually conceived as a tricky old man who, if caught, may reveal the hiding place of treasure. This one certainly looks as if he had a secret.

Place the white fur as indicated in the accompanying illustration with the first piece low on the egg and another strip just above this so you will have the illusion of long hair. This should be clipped so it will be flush with the foot of the glass when the head is placed on it. Since I wanted this head to have a little more height, I glued it to the cap of a spirits bottle and this cap was glued to the foot of the glass.

After the hair has been glued on as directed, you will have a bald spot at the top. Do not cover this. Paint the ears flesh color (pink and white mixed with a tiny bit of brown) and glue them on the sides of the head.

Cut a strip of fur about ¼-inch wide. Clip short and fit across the forehead, making it long enough to cover the lower part of the ears. You'll have to measure, as egg sizes differ.

After you have drawn on the face and painted it, cut two pieces of fur to be placed low on either side of the cheeks and a third piece to fit across the chin to form a beard.

The hat, made of green felt, should now be affixed on the head with contact glue. Your charming little sprite is now complete.

The three Kings from the East are all made in very much the same way, differing only in hair color and headdresses.

The first king is the youngest and has black hair parted in the center and clipped to about the length young men wear their hair today. He has a neat black mustache made of two tiny pieces of fur clipped to the

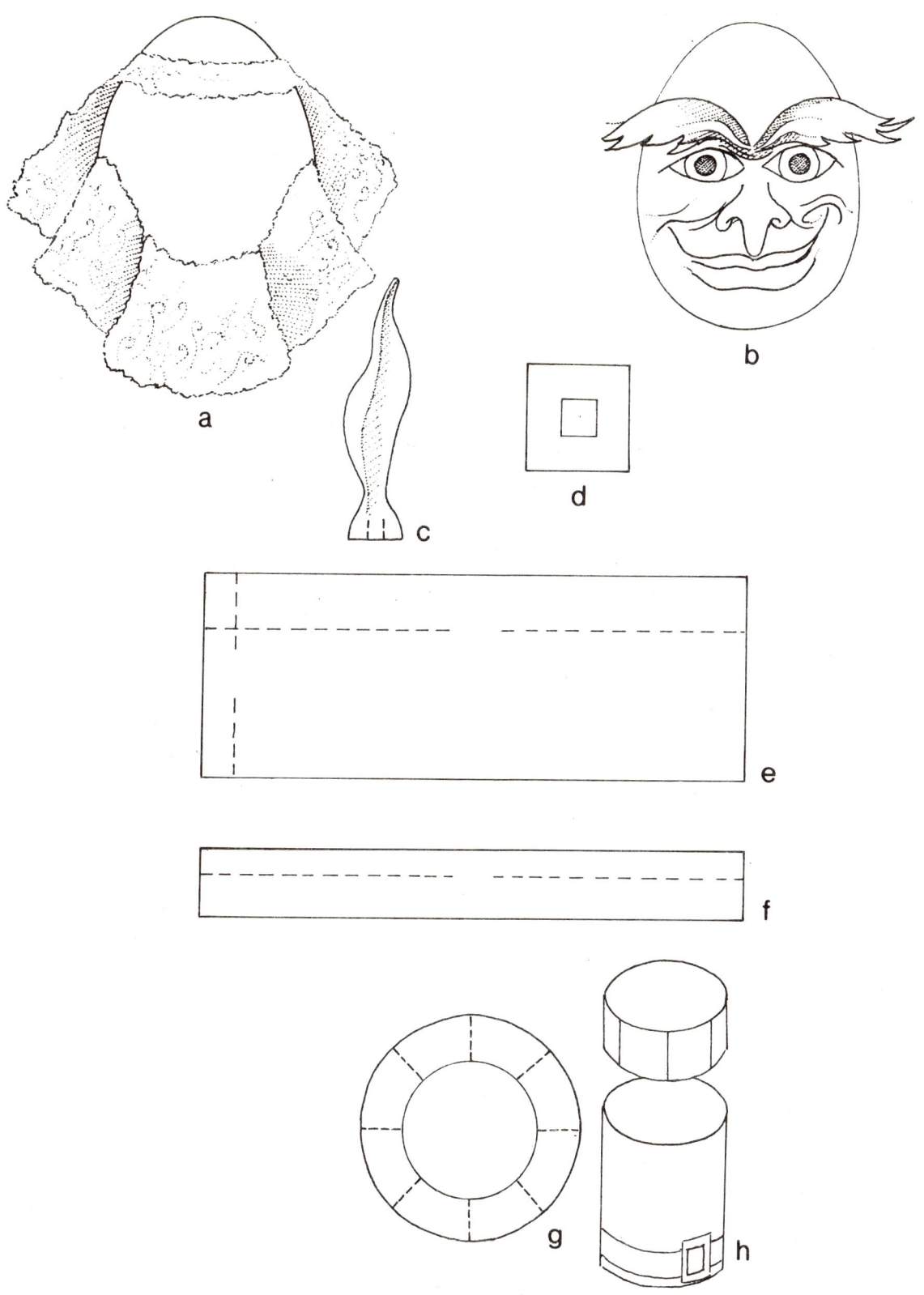

Making a Leprechaun: a) cut fur for head; b) paint features; c) cut ears and paste on; d) cut buckle; e)f) cut paper for top (1½" X 5½") and hat band (¼" X 5¾"). Cover these with green felt; g) cut hat top, 2" diameter; h) assemble hat.

right proportion to look well on the face. Another small piece has been clipped and put just under the pleasant but unsmiling mouth to form a pointed black beard. The eyes and eyebrows are painted black. The nostrils are outlined in black and the mouth is painted a brown-red.

The crown was made from a strip of gold braid to which I fastened several small circles cut from a paper doily and painted with gold Liquid Leaf. A pin of "pearls" and "emeralds" decorated the front. Rhinestones set into the crown at intervals would work very well.

The second king (not shown) is very similar to the first, but I gave this one dark brown hair and placed a small piece of striped silk cloth on his head before setting on the crown—in the fashion of the hooded mantle called a burnoose worn by the Arabs.

The third king (also not shown) has white hair, a long, flowing white beard and blue eyes. Crown and hooded mantle are blue touched with gold and the crown is set with blue rhinestones.

Lastly we have an amusing pair—a young bride and groom.

The young man wears his hair in the fashion of today with sideburns and a smart, clipped mustache. Eyes are brown, outlined in black and the black eyebrows were done with short strokes of my crow quill pen dipped in black India ink.

His darling, golden-haired bride is very modest with downcast eyes and a pleasant pink rosebud mouth.

The bright yellow fake fur hair was set on to form a side part and pulled to the back into a tight, tiny roll. I sewed the roll with matching thread and firmly glued it down to the back of the head and then sprayed it to keep it in place.

The young lady's veil was made of 15 inches of fine nylon net two inches wide. After this was gathered with a $1/4$-inch heading, I sewed a row of 3-mm. pearl beads to the net. Another strand of pearl beads (about 20 in number) was brought forward to be placed in a half circle over the front.

Both bride and groom heads were set in gold plastic curtain rings and affixed to the champagne glasses.

I find the eggheads so much fun that it is difficult for me to leave them. Some day when I have time I hope to make up a whole set of little animals. Another enchanting idea would be little girls of all nations with appropriate features, expressions, and headdresses. Wouldn't a little Chinese girl be a real doll? Or perhaps one with the typical Siamese headdress, or a small African.... But these must wait, for now we go on to the "leather clad Westerns."

CHAPTER SEVEN

Leather-Clad Western Eggs

The Western eggs are, as far as I can determine, unique and though they may look difficult, they really are not. Leather of the soft, garment type is very easy to work with.

For reasons which will be obvious later on, I started this project with a large turkey egg from which I cut away about 1/3 of the shell so that the egg forms an "alcove." I laid the shell on a piece of yellow leather large enough to cover it. Leather has no bias so it does not matter in which direction it is cut; just be sure your piece is large enough. Glue down the back, then the top, bottom, and sides. You will now have four little peaks of leather sticking up.

Taking one section at a time, cut off the excess leather and glue the cut edges down to the egg. Dry well between each section so the leather will not pull out of place. Though the decoration varies with each egg, this method of applying the leather is the same for all. It must be gently tugged and pulled into place for a smooth fit. If you have places where the leather bunches up (pieces of leather are not always of a uniform thickness like cloth), you may need to make some small additional cuts, trimming off more leather and gluing down as you go.

I chose a turkey egg for my Indian cradle because of a legend among the Choctaws that when a boy baby is born, his parents should rub his feet with a turkey claw so that he will become a "swift runner"—something greatly admired by all the tribes.

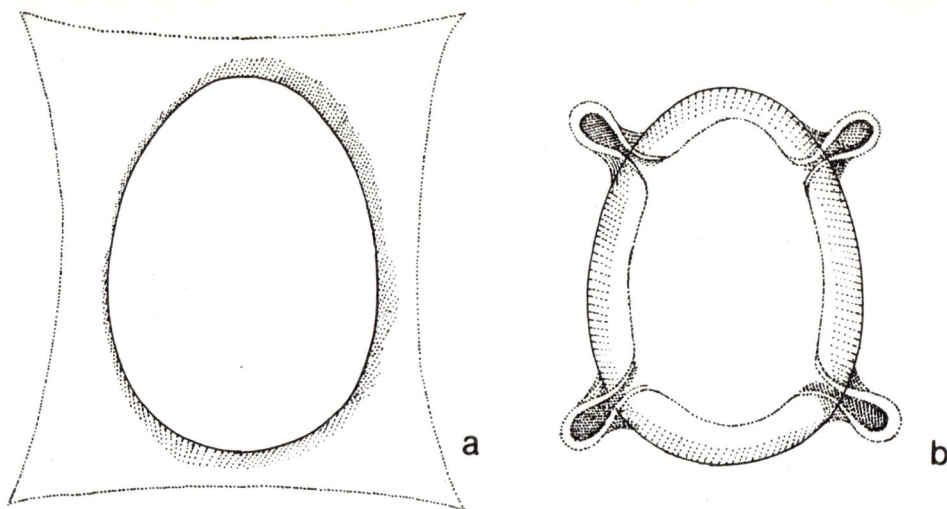

After the yellow leather covering was dry, I decorated the back of the egg with 12 strips of blue leather placed so the yellow leather would show through in alternating stripes. The ends of the blue leather strips (each one about 1/4-inch wide) were cut to form points, and the points would center on the lower back part of the egg.

At the front, the outer rim of the egg is edged with a tiny, 1/8-inch strip of brown leather.

A strip of red leather 1/4-inch wide, was placed around the rim of the shell *inside* the egg, just at the edge of the brown rim.

Another strip of red leather was glued around the outer edge of the egg, just behind the brown leather—this strip also 1/4-inch wide.

Next, I laid the egg face downward on a piece of red leather and traced around it with a pencil. I cut out the oval on the line, leaving the rest of the leather intact. Then, leaving about 1 1/4 inches all around, I cut around the hole (in the leather) conforming to the shape of the egg. The sides were then slashed about 1/2-inch deep at the outer edge to form a fringe.

This red leather "halo" was then glued just back of the 1/4-inch piece of red leather on the outside front of the egg. Use contact glue for this and you will find you can make a very neat fit. The leather halo is also stiff enough to stand up well without any additional backing.

Prepare the stand by taking an empty thread spool one inch in diameter, and covering it with a strip of blue leather. At the top edge, glue on a strip of red leather 1/4-inch wide. On the top of the spool place 1/2-inch diameter white plastic curtain ring and glue. This will form a receptacle for the curved bottom of the egg.

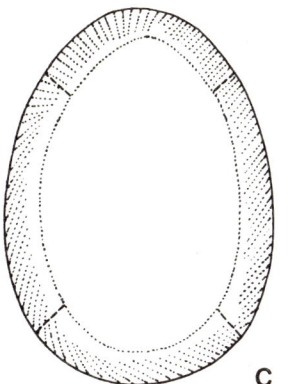 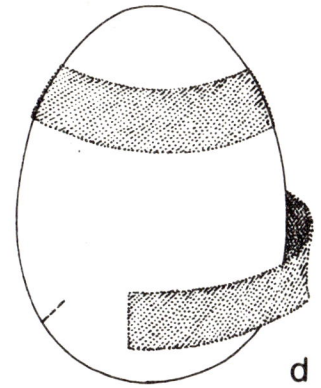 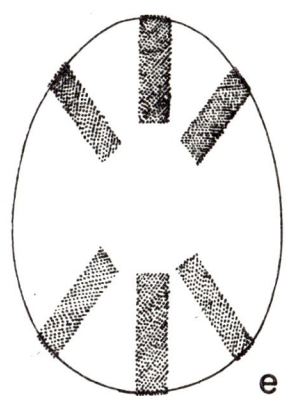

Making leather-clad eggs: a) Glue leather to eggs at top, bottom and sides; b) snip off peaks; c) glue cut edges down to the egg; d) cuts may be covered at back of egg with ¼-inch strips, draped so two slashes are covered by each piece; e) Or cuts may be covered in this way.

Next take a small jar lid, about 2 inches in diameter, and cover the top with a piece of yellow leather cut to fit. Run a strip of red leather, ¼-inch wide, around the edge. The spool should then be glued to the top of the lid.

Trace and cut a tiny thunderbird of red leather (the thunderbird is a design that traditionally belongs to all the Indian tribes of the Southwest) and glue this to the front of the leather-covered spool.

After setting the egg in the curtain ring I began the beadwork.

Use a row of blue beads, one by one, around the brown leather rim of the egg, followed by two rows of white beads as shown, one on the red leather rim back of the brown, and the other on the red leather "halo" itself.

On the egg stand, I used green and yellow beads on the upper edge of the red leather rim, white beads on the thunderbird, and a row of red around the lower edges of the blue leather.

Use a row of blue beads where the yellow leather of the lid and the red leather of the rim join, and a row of white beads on the lower rim of the lid. The beads used are all "pony" beads, which are slightly larger than seed beads.

The interior of the turkey egg was purposely left in its natural color for contrast with the papoose which is dressed in brown leather.

Because I could not find a small Indian baby doll I painted the face of a tiny 1½-inch doll I found at the dime store with light brown acrylic paint and darkened the blue eyes to dark brown and made the fair hair dark. If you cannot find a doll like this in one of your local stores several mail order houses that offer cake-decorating supplies have

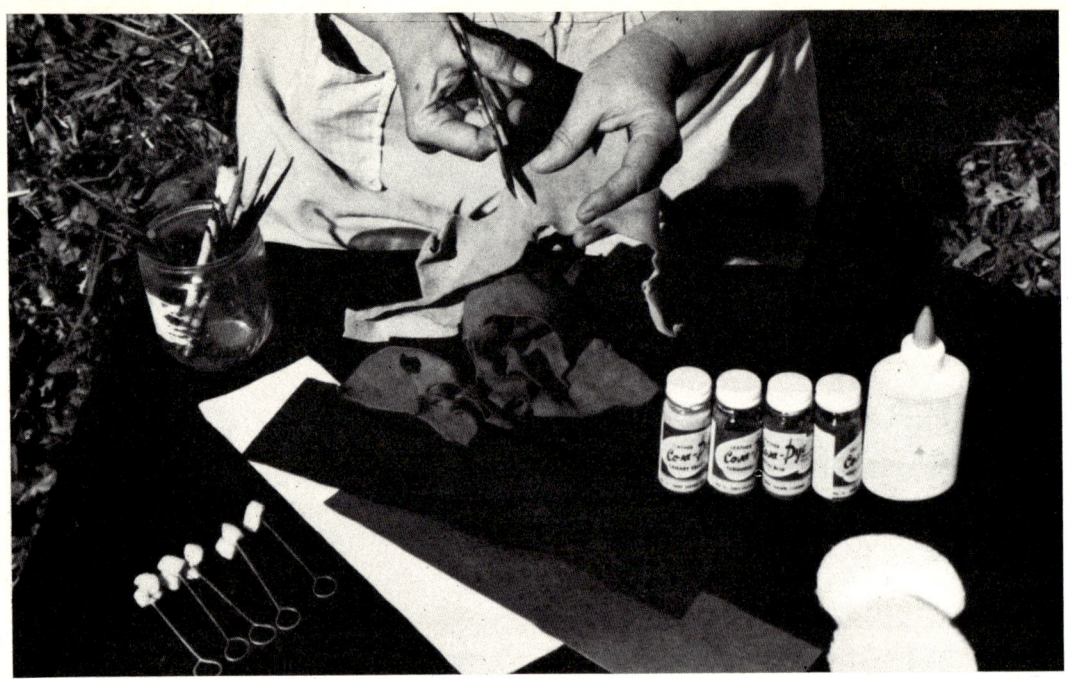

Garment-type leather is easily cut with ordinary scissors.

them. They are usually about 1⅛-inches long.

To clothe the papoose, cut a strip of brown leather about two inches long and one inch wide. Gather on one of the long edges (with needle and thread), sew the wide edges together, and pull over the head to form a little hood. The bottom is then pulled down over the shoulders like a little cape.

Lay the doll on another small piece of brown leather and cut just to meet at the front where the leather should be sewn together with light tan thread, crossing over and back again to simulate lacing. Trim the lower part of this piece of leather just to cover the feet and then pull the bottom together tightly by sewing with dark brown thread.

After the brown leather "clothes" of the little papoose have been decorated with blue, white, and red beads, the little figure is placed in the egg. Glue so figure will stand upright.

Now I realize that the designs for these Western eggs call for leather in many different colors and many of you may not find all the colors easy to come by.

Red, black, brown, tan, and white are much used and are generally easy to find as garments are frequently cut from these and scraps large enough for the eggs can often be purchased from garment factories or even in shoe shops which repair leather goods.

Blue, yellow, green, etc. may not be so easy to find so I simply dye them myself, starting with a piece of white leather.

Prepare the leather for dyeing by using a cleaning compound. You can mix your own. Dissolve one teaspoon of oxalic acid crystals (obtainable at drug stores) in a pint of water. Or, if you prefer, you can use one of the prepared leather cleaners such as Cove Dye Remover and Deglazer made by Tandy Leather Company. This is used to prepare leather for dyeing and also to remove dirt and wax.

For coloring there are two types of dye available. Omega Dye is oil and spirit solvent and water-resistant. It is also permanent, penetrates deeply, and will dye the leather evenly and uniformly. The colors can all be intermixed and thinned. Omega Dye comes in black, light brown, dark brown, blue, tan, red, medium brown, cordovan and green. These are all dark, rich colors and are obtainable in four-ounce jars.

If you decide to work with Omega Dye you should use a small felt applicator. Practice first on a scrap of leather dipping the applicator in the desired color. Start working in the upper left hand corner and move with a quick, circular motion so each stroke will just slightly overlap the previous one.

As the color on the applicator is used, dip into the dye and keep working until your piece of leather is entirely covered. Let dry thoroughly for an hour or two, depending on weather conditions. The leather will dry more quickly on a warm day and with corresponding slowness on a humid one.

Do not be dismayed if you note lighter or darker spots. These are due to the heavier penetration of the dye into the leather where the applicator first touched it. Your dye job will probably be quite uneven after the first application. Usually it is necessary to repeat the dye job at least three times before the color and evenness wanted is achieved.

Garment leather is obtainable in a number of different type skins such as sheer lambskin suede, garment cabretta, New Zealand lambskin (this comes in Aztec turquoise as well as black, brown, copper and wheat beige), reversible garment sides, etc. Reversible garment sides can be purchased in white.

Cova is the other type of dye and the one I most frequently use for I find it easier. Though it is less durable, it will go on smoothly and quickly with little or no streaking. Also, while it is water-soluble when wet, it is waterproof when dry, making it easy to clean. It can be counted on to cover all leathers (except suedes and patents). You can even cover old colors and, with patience, turn black to white.

Cova may be had in nine brilliant shades: canary yellow, royal blue, medium brown, kelly green, white, light brown, turquoise, jubilee red and midnight black. These colors come in one-ounce bottles.

For water dyes I dislike using the cotton swabs or shearling I use for the Omega because they tend to hold back the color solids. I find it easiest and most practical to use a large, flat lettering brush. The camel-hair brushes are preferable as they are soft and nonstreaking. The best size, designed for smooth, even strokes is ¼-inch wide.

Remember to wash your brushes thoroughly each time you use them so no dye will remain on the bristles. Use mild soap and water. Dry and shape your brush after washing and stand it up in a jar or bottle, bristle end up, so they will remain in place.

Even with Cova dye I often find it necessary to use several applications before I obtain the shade I want. Always use horizontal and diagonal strokes when dyeing with the lettering brush for the second and third applications as this will generally result in a more even coloring job.

After the desired shade is reached, be sure you allow the leather to dry thoroughly before cutting; usually half an hour with water dye is all that is necessary. (Note: Plastic gloves, thin enough to give you complete freedom of movement, are nice to use when working with leather dyes to protect your hands.)

Here is something else you should remember. Leather, even from the same tannery, will vary and may produce a slightly different shade of the same color, due to chemical changes during the tanning process. So, if you are planning to cover several eggs and want them all to be the same color, cut all the pieces from the same piece of leather.

Also, if you intend to dye in quantity have an adequate supply of dye (from one container) on hand sufficient to complete all the dyeing. Sometimes the same color, from the same manufacturer—in a different lot shipment—will produce different shades.

As with all things, a certain amount of individual experimenting may be necessary before you find that you can get the desired results in your dyeing process.

You may also want to try dilution of your colors to make soft pastel shades. Or, perhaps, cross-dyeing to add to your color "wardrobe." For instance, red dyed over blue will make purple or violet, depending on whether or not you have diluted your colors. Yellow over red will give you orange-red or bright vermillion.

After the leather is dyed you will experience no more difficulty in cutting it than before. Garment leather is soft, light in weight, pliable, and will cut easily with ordinary scissors. Use your sewing scissors and keep a pair of small curved blade scissors handy for cutting very tiny pieces. A pair of decoupage scissors with straight blades may also be useful.

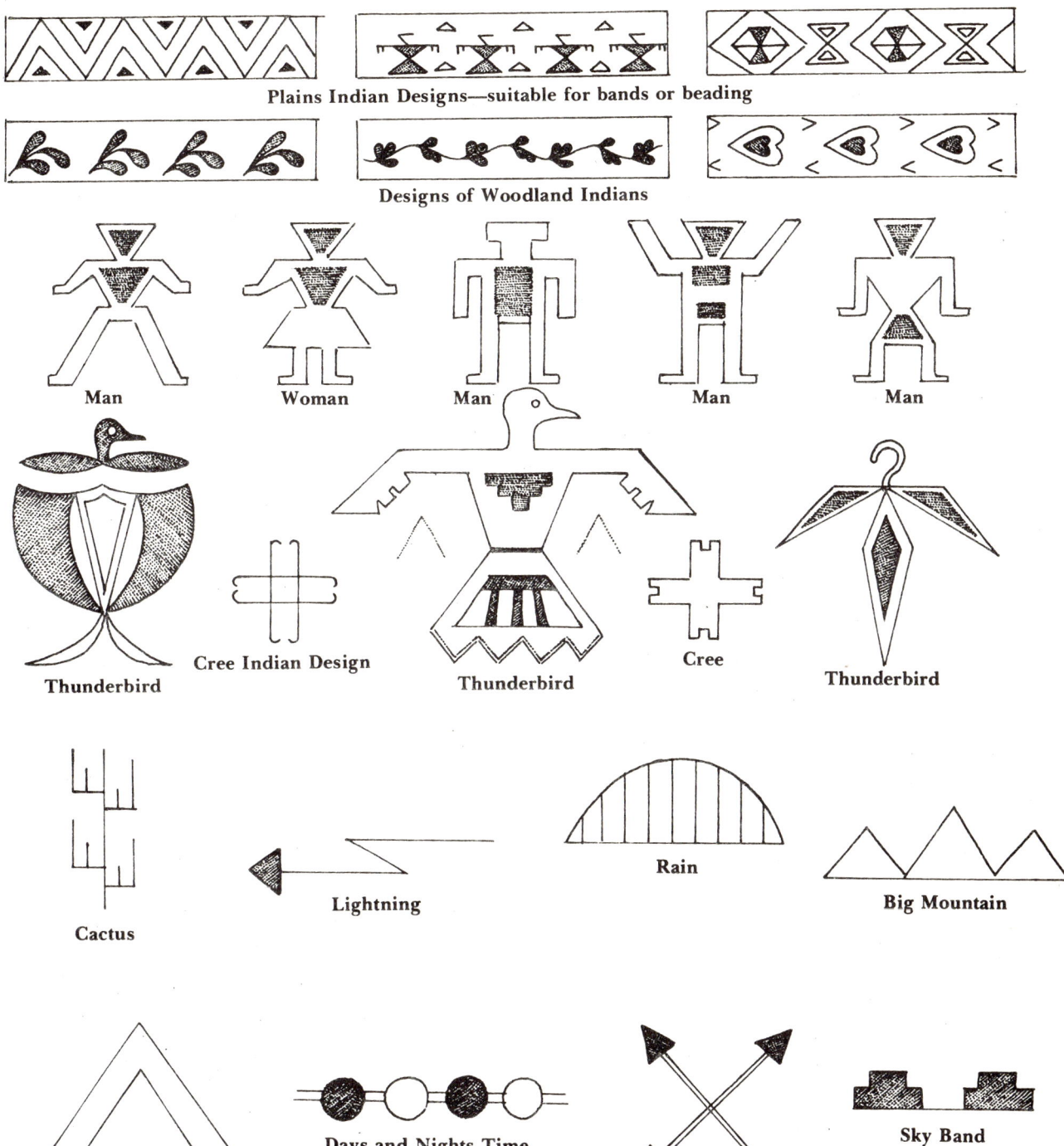

Seed beads and the slightly larger pony beads are obtainable almost everywhere but you might find it fun to order your beads at the same supply house where the Plains Indians of Oklahoma buy theirs.

While on a visit to Anadarko, Oklahoma, several years ago I bought a supply of beads at Indian City, U.S.A. This village, two and one-half miles southeast of Anadarko is a re-creation of seven ancient Indian dwellings and artifacts. The address for Indian City and other bead supply houses is given in the listing at the back of this book.

Indians are intensely down-to-earth and practical, and most of their designs are things they are familiar with in their everyday life. A disk will stand for the sun, a triangle or semicircle for rain, a zig-zag for lightning, and days and nights are black and white beads strung on a cord.

For decorating the Western leather-clad eggs you may use either chicken, turkey, duck or goose eggs, depending on the scene you have chosen to portray.

For my cowboy on his horse swinging a lasso I chose a well-rounded chicken egg and covered it with light tan leather. This forms the back and I crossed two ¼-inch pieces over this to cover the cuts made in the leather which were necessary to shape it to conform to the rounded contours of the egg.

I used two pieces of leather for the opening of the egg, each cut ¼-inch wide and long enough to follow the curve of the egg. These were glued, one on the inside and one on the outside.

You will have a very narrow space, less than ⅛-inch wide, between the two strips of leather. To cover this, string a sufficient number of red pony beads (these are just a little larger than seed beads) to go around and fit into this small space. When you have enough, glue them in place and snip the thread drawing and glue it under so that it will not show. Catch the beads quickly as you do this so they will not fall off.

Now, just behind and adjacent to the red beads, place a strand of red and blue beads, alternating in color, three and three.

Cut the frame or "halo" of medium-brown leather by laying the egg face downward on your leather and drawing around it so you will have the exact size for your frame. Allow one inch all around when you cut out the frame, slashing about ¾-inch deep to form the fringe.

Using contact glue, run a thread of glue all around the outside brown leather rim previously placed on the egg, and fit the leather frame to it, holding the frame upright for a few minutes until the glue begins to set. The leather is stiff enough so it will stand in position without any additional backing.

Let this dry well before you proceed.

Next run a strand of beads (blue and red alternating in threes) around the joint of the two pieces of leather, snipping the thread when you have enough and gluing down as before.

In front of this strand run a string of all-white beads.

In front of the all-white beads run a string of blue and yellow beads, alternating in threes.

When this is all dry, the frame should be decorated by gluing on two rows of beads, one blue and one red. These are glued on separately and are placed a tiny distance from each other.

The stand for this egg began as a small, round, polished wood salt shaker. At the top there is a small white plastic curtain ring to which the bottom of the egg is glued. Around this, where it joins the wood base, I ran a string of red and blue beads, alternating in threes.

At the bottom of the base, which is set in a gold plastic curtain ring (1½ inches diameter), are two strands of pony beads, one red and yellow and the lower one all-white.

For my tiny Western cowboy, I went to the children's section of the dime store, found a figure I liked of the right dimensions, and bought the package of little plastic figures which contained a number of cowboys and horses in different attitudes and colors.

The horse, which was already black, I left unpainted. The cowboy needed touching up and, using acrylic paint, I gave him brown skin, gray-tan chaps (chaparajos, overalls of leather, usually open at the back, worn by cowboys as a protection against thorns) to simulate cowhide, gray hat and shirt, and a red neckerchief. This was a working cowboy and these were working clothes.

The interior of the egg was left undecorated, the natural white forming a good background for the little figure.

For my Indian with the bow and arrow, I used a large duck egg, as this figure, also bought at the dime store, is larger and I needed the additional height which this egg gave me.

This figure I also had to repaint to tone down the original colors. The skin was painted a coppery brown, the trousers tan to look like bucksin; the moccasins and quiver I painted blue, black for the hair and red for the feathers. I even put tiny streaks of red and white on the face to simulate war paint, using my No. 1 Grumbacher camel-hair brush to do this.

I left the interior of the egg its natural white, running a ¼-inch rim of red leather around the inside and adding a small, triangular piece of red leather where the Indian stands.

I used a strip of tan leather braid for the exterior rim of the egg. This may be purchased at fabric shops and gives a very neat finish to these eggs. You can get needles made especially for sewing leather at the Singer shops, but I usually find the garment leather so soft that it will sew with an ordinary sewing needle of large size.

For the small space between the red leather on the inside of the egg and the light tan leather on the outside of the egg, I beaded a string of all-dark blue beads and fastened them down to cover the rim of the egg.

The frame for this egg is of bright blue leather cut to fit, shaped and fringed as before. It is narrower at the sides, to conform to the shape of the egg and a slight peak at the top gives additional height.

After the frame was glued and dried, I ran a string of red pony beads around the joining point, following this with a string of all-white which contrasted nicely with the blue of the frame.

The stand for this egg is the cap from a liquor bottle glued to a small (1¾-inch) lid from a cosmetic jar.

Cover the rim of the lid with a strip of blue leather and the top with a piece of red. (Lay cap on leather, draw around with pencil, and cut.)

Cover the cap of the spirits bottle with yellow and set a white plastic curtain ring on top.

Cut tiny strips of red leather and place them diagonally (making Vs) on the yellow cap, finishing top and bottom with narrow strips of leather (about ⅛-inch wide). This is to simulate a war drum.

Run a strand of dark blue pony beads around the white curtain ring.

Run a strand of white beads, followed by a strand of blue beads, around the drum where it stands on the red leather lid.

Run a strand of all-white beads around the base of the lid.

When the stand is completed and dry, position the egg on a curtain ring and glue firmly with contact adhesive.

The friend who gave me the "Kachina Doll" for my next Western egg project told me it was originally a pendant for a piece of Sarah Coventry jewelry. It could well be for it is exquisitely made with silver wire, pearls, and red and turquoise beads.

Whatever purpose it may have served originally, it suggested the Kachina dolls of the Southwest. These dolls, of carved wood, figure prominently in the ceremonies of the Hopi—the Pueblo Indians of Arizona.

They are often spoken of as "gods" but actually are not worshipped— and you must understand the Indians and their way of life to know the meaning of their attitude toward them. They consider them to be the personification of supernatural beings, spirits who hold the powers of life and who appear among them from time to time as honored visitors and to give assistance.

Kachina dolls are religious symbols of the Hopi Indians of the Southwest. This one is suspended, so it "dances" when it is picked up.

Hopi men, dressed like Kachinas, perform dramatic ceremonial dances at the winter and spring festivals. Traditionally, the dolls, which are used in the dances, also wear the costumes of the dancers. These may be the Eagle Spirit, the Owl Spirit, the Warrior God Kachina, and hundreds of others. After the ceremonies are over, the children of the tribe are given the dolls to play with.

Giving these to the children is not thought of as being in any way disrespectful—rather it is considered a method of teaching the youngsters about these beings who have in centuries past formed their daily lives through the Indians' belief in their existence.

To house my Kachina doll, I chose a large, round chicken egg, carefully selected so the Kachina could hang by a tiny strip of leather from the top and still have room to "dance" around when the egg was lifted up to be looked at, or held in the hand.

The interior of the egg was left unpainted, the natural pearly white forming a good background for the little jeweled figure.

A strip of white leather, ¼-inch wide, was run around the rim of the egg inside and a similar strip, also ¼-inch wide, around the exterior rim.

Where the eggshell rim showed between the two strips of white leather, I ran a strand of all-red pony beads, gluing them in place.

The halo of white leather was cut and firmly glued just behind the white leather strip on the exterior rim of the egg and allowed to dry.

Where the two leather strips were glued together, I placed a strand of all-red pony beads and just in front of them a strand of red and yellow pony beads (three and three of each color).

On the white leather halo itself, I glued two rows of individual turquoise beads about ⅛-inch apart.

The stand for this was made in exactly the same way as the one for the little cowboy on his horse, using the pepper shaker this time.

Not all the Indian legends come from the West. One of the loveliest comes to us from the Saranac Indians of what is now New York State, and concerns the Lake of Clustered Stars.

Like so many tribal legends, it is a tale of love and centers around the beautiful lake (now called Tupper Lake) on whose shores the lovers were finally reunited. I have chosen this lake for my next theme. Here the beautiful white swans swim in serene waters as they did long ago on the Lake of Clustered Stars when the Indians lived nearby. They are surrounded by trees and flowers which the Indians call "Tokens of Love from Great Spirit."

Begin with a large goose egg, cutting away about one third of the shell so that it will have an oval alcove shape.

Cover the egg with soft black garment leather, pulling it flat to conform to the shape of the shell and cutting in the four areas (or more), necessary to make it fit. Cover the cuts with strips of black leather about ¼ inch wide so the slashes will not be apparent and edge these strips with strands of red beads.

For the decoration on this egg, I beaded a strip on my Indian beading loom in a red and white alternating pattern as shown in the picture, the design being a simple block and triangle five beads wide.

Here is how the loom is made: nail two small blocks of wood to a base as shown in the illustration. The base should be about 18 inches long and 3 inches wide, the blocks about 2½ inches high and 3 inches wide.

Next, hammer a row of eight small finishing nails (more if you would do a wider piece of work) ¼-inch apart on the top of each wooden

The Lake of Clustered Stars, a favorite Indian theme, with white swans swimming on a tiny mirror.

block. Cut seven strands of waxed thread (use beeswax if you can get it), about eight inches longer than the piece you are planning to bead.

Place a large nail on each end of the base. Tie threads on one end nail and spread threads between the small nails across the top of the blocks, tying them firmly on the end nail on the opposite side.

Thread your needle (use a special beading needle) and tie end of thread on front warp thread. String six beads on the needle thread. (If you are planning a piece with five beads use six threads; for seven beads you would use eight threads, etc.) Lay the threaded beads underneath your loom threads, pressing them upward with your fingers and spacing them evenly between the strings.

Holding them in position from below, put your needle over the back warp thread and through each bead, from the back forward, over the threads. This will hold the beads in place. Repeat the procedure for each row.

For a simple design of two colors you can usually count the beads of each color as you weave them, but a more intricate design of several

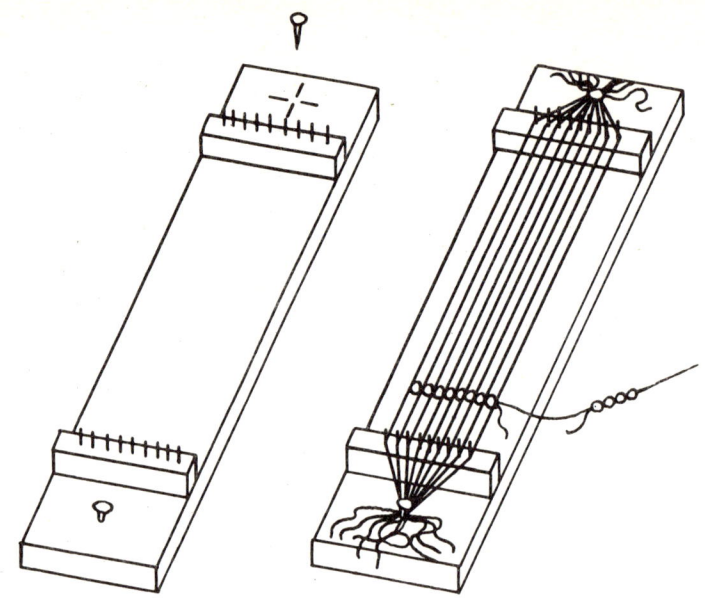

Using the beading loom: Begin as shown below. Hold beads in place on underside of warp and bring thread over end warp thread and back through beads above the warp. Repeat for each row.

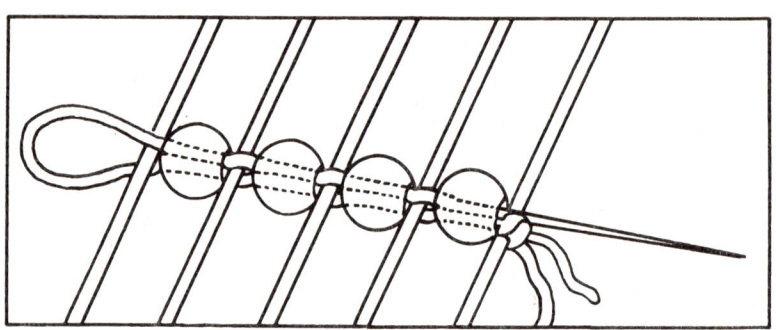

colors should be planned and designed on a sheet of paper. This will give you a better idea of how the different colors will harmonize.

It is best not to make these bands too wide when they are to be used for decorating the eggshell openings, as the narrower ones go on more smoothly.

Having completed your piece of beadwork to the desired length, fasten the ends and remove from loom. Measure beadwork by placing it around the egg opening to be sure it will fit. It is better to have it a little too long than too short. If it is a fractional bit too long just cut carefully and glue down to the leather immediately so the beads will stay in place. If a bit short, glue on extra beads to match the pattern.

Three strands of beads, two red and one blue, are then added at the shell opening to cover the edge of the leather.

Following the method previously described, a halo for this egg is cut by laying it open side down on a piece of heavy saddle leather (6 to 7 ounce cowhide). To cut this leather, I used a pair of heavy scissors, first drawing the design outline with a lead pencil so it would be accurately proportioned.

Since this saddle leather is heavier than the garment leather, I did not fringe it as I had done with the others but decided to tool it instead with my Craftool Steel Leather stamps (purchasable at Tandy Leather Company).

Decorating leather by carving is one of the most beautiful and timeless forms of decorating and this carving should be done before the hood or halo is put on the egg.

Begin "casing" the leather by submerging it in water momentarily, then lay it grain-side (this is the smooth, hair side of the leather; the "flesh" side is the underpart) up until the water evaporates and the leather is almost its natural color.

Or you can wet the leather from the flesh side, using a sponge and then run the sponge over the grain side. Again, let the leather return to almost its natural color.

If necessary, you may dampen some parts of the leather which may dry out before you finish decorating it. Additional moisture may be applied to the top or grain side with a damp sponge as needed.

Be sure always to use a porcelain, glass, or enameled container when casing leather, as metal will stain wet leather.

For best results a tooling board or a similar smooth, hard-surfaced piece of material should be used when working with stamping tools. The design I have used is a simple, geometrical one using my tools No. 366, No. 431, No. 202, No. 104, and No. 105.

I used my Select-A-Stroke mallet which has a 9-ounce head. This, or a similar mallet, should always be used as the striking force on decorating stamping tools for it will never chip the tools and will last indefinitely. Never use a metal hammer.

To use the mallet, hold both the mallet and the decorative stamping tool almost perpendicular. It should be held securely, but do not be tense for this will tire you—relax and enjoy your work.

The mallet should be held in the center of the handle for the best balance, holding it mostly with your fingers, rather than the palm of your hand. If you want deep depressions, hold the mallet handle more nearly toward the end but try to be as comfortable as possible, perhaps trying several positions to see which suits you best.

Always stamp the impressions away from you. This will make the impressions easier to see and give you better control. And try to space the impressions as evenly as possible.

Of course, there are a great many techniques to be employed in stamping leather, some very intricate, but for a simple decorating project such as I have outlined we will not need to go into all of these.

After my design has been stamped out, the leather frame is glued to the eggshell just behind the strip of loomed beading.

Cover the joining point with a strand of blue pony beads with another row of white pony beads placed around and behind the blue ones.

The interior of the egg (and for this egg I used one of those described in the next chapter, from which the membrane was removed and discarded) was painted with black acrylic.

On the black background I glued seven clustered white rhinestone trim stars.

For the "lake" I used a tiny round mirror which was set in plaster. At the back of the egg is a tiny, green plastic pine tree.

In the foreground swims a graceful white swan with her two cygnets. The plaster which shows around the tiny lake is painted green.

The stand for this egg is made of ceramic and was purchased at a ceramic shop. It was white, having been fired in the kiln, but not colored.

To make a larger base to balance better with the rather large leather frame, I set the ceramic egg holder in the flat, lower portion of a small 2-inch powder jar base.

The ceramic egg stand and the base were both painted with gold Liquid Leaf and then antiqued. When dry, the decorated egg was securely glued to the ceramic stand by using contact glue.

CHAPTER EIGHT

Cutting the Eggshells

One of the reasons I find egg decoration so great both as a hobby and, occasionally, to make money is because it is such an inexpensive craft. I am simply an "everyday" housewife—I do not have many special tools —my studio is my kitchen table.

I do, however, have one tool which I simply could not do without— my Dremel Moto-Tool, used for cutting the heavy-shelled goose eggs and the durable guinea eggs which make such unusual and attractive decorations but need a special cutting tool to penetrate.

Many of my designs use chicken or duck eggs and these can be cut with a pair of manicure or decoupage scissors, though not so neatly. These eggs have thinner shells so it's easier to pierce them. Many of the decorated eggs are not cut at all, just blown out and used whole.

You do not have to invest in this tool unless you want to cut goose eggs or make the eggs which are not covered by some type of material. Eggs that are covered by leather or velvet will have the slightly rough edges hidden. For these I often just use the breakfast eggs.

Begin by making a hole in the egg at about the middle, enlarge it carefully so it will admit curved blade scissors, and merrily cut away. Depending on the way you want to use the egg, you will have about ½ or ⅓ of the shell which you will have no immediate use for. Do not throw this away; wash it along with the larger piece and when it is dry put it away in a container. Do this also with any eggshells you inadvertently break in the cutting process. I have a surprise coming up later on, for even these broken shells can be made into beautiful egg decorations for a great many objects.

Let's face it: eggshells, like so many other things, are simply not what they used to be. The eggs that most of us obtain at the grocery stores are pretty thin-shelled indeed.

Since we have little or no control over the way the eggshells are produced, the best we can do is to find ways to strengthen the shells artificially. There are several ways of doing this.

One way is to spray the egg (chicken or duck egg) with three coats of acrylic paint (white or clear). Let the egg dry well between coats. Then, beginning in the center of the egg, make a hole with a small nail or corsage pin and cut out a piece about the size of a quarter which will permit the contents to be drained into a bowl without breaking the yolk.

Now, cut the hole large enough so you can wash the egg well, but not as large as you intend the final opening to be. Let the egg dry and spray the inside, as you did the outside, with three coats of the acrylic paint.

When the inside is completely dry, using curved blade manicure scissors, enlarge the hole to the shape you want. This method takes a little time and patience, but the results are worthwhile as the edges will be relatively smooth and free from the jaggedness of the untreated shells.

Other sprays and paints such as shellac or enamels will also strengthen the shells and you may find through experimentation that other preparations will work well to enable your cutting operations to go more smoothly.

So much for chicken and duck eggs. When it comes to cutting the goose eggs, I really enjoy using my Dremel Moto-Tool, which is a rotary grinding tool. The precision work it will do is just not possible to achieve in any other way—at least it is not so easy. And if you do decide to get one (see list of suppliers for address of manufacturer) it will save a lot of time and trouble in cutting chicken and duck eggs, too.

To start, you must decide upon the design of the egg you are planning to decorate. I find it easiest simply to draw this on the egg with a lead pencil. For those of you who find drawing difficult, there is a small device which you may like to use.

The Dremel, which has many other uses besides cutting eggshells, comes with a number of different attachments. The one I prefer to use for cutting shells is the cutting wheel, No. 409. This is an emery wheel for slicing, cutting off and similar operations. The dental tool (small No. 125

Cutting egg shells with tool.

burr) may be used for drilling holes in the ends of the eggs when the whole egg is wanted.

A word of caution. Always be very careful to unplug your Moto-Tool when changing collets (four collets are available, each has a different hole diameter in order to accept various accessory shanks or inserting accessories). Read the instructions carefully or have your dealer show you how to use the tool. It is important that only a full wave output speed control like the Dremel Model 219 be used.

When you first start using the Dremel you may find the finger grip attachment will aid you in doing precise work. It is included as part of the kit and slips easily onto the front of the motor casing and is helpful when doing close tolerance work.

Another word of caution. It is important that you protect your eyes when grinding or routing with the Moto-Tool by always wearing safety glasses. While I always observe this rule, I have actually experienced little difficulty with flying particles when cutting eggshells since they mostly seem to just disintegrate into tiny particles of dust. There is a slight burning odor as you cut, but this is not disagreeable and quickly disappears.

Some of the shapes into which eggs may be cut are shown in the illustration. Perhaps the easiest cut to start with is the one I call the "alcove" cut, which may be a simple oval, or the heart shape I have used for several of my decorated eggs, cutting away about 1/3 of the shell.

If you want to make eggs where the shell is cut approximately in half and the two sections are secured with a hinge, you should begin by drawing your pencil lines showing where the cuts are to be made.

Mark the line first where the shell is to be cut in half. Mark for the hinge by laying the hinge on the egg with the hinge pin on the cutting line. Trace with a pencil all the way around the hinge.

When you start your actual cutting, be sure to work over a padded table. Several large bath towels will work just fine.

Start by cutting from right to left and try not to penetrate the shell too deeply with the blade, using the outer edge of the blade only. It will be easiest if you start cutting at the center of the egg rather than at one of the ends.

When you have cut the shell about 3/4 of the way around, hold only half the egg, allowing the remaining half to fall away and the contents of the egg to drop into a bowl.

You do not have to hold the egg over a bowl when you first start cutting; in fact it is a lot easier not to do so. After you have cut an egg or two you will know *when* to place the egg over a receptacle and you will find a shallow pan or bowl most convenient.

After the egg is cut open, empty the contents immediately, so you will have a clean membrane. This membrane should be finger-smoothed to prevent air pockets. When it dries it will have an attractive pearly sheen and will stick to the egg. For some decorated eggs, such as the Westerns, this will make an attractive background.

To cut the notch for the hinge, the slot on each half of the shell should be only half the depth of the rounded part of the hinge. Try the hinge for size and don't make your cut too long.

Before the hinge is glued on the egg, you should make sure that it works easily and smoothly. There are several ways to do this. A good soaking in machine oil (such as you use for oiling your sewing machine) may be all that is necessary. If this doesn't work, try prying open the crimped portion of the hinge with a small screwdriver. Small hinges can be purchased at craft shops; I found mine at an office supply store which also deals in craft supplies.

The eggs we are talking about here are *good* eggs in prime condition. Maybe you find you can't get good eggs. Goose eggs, in some localities, are especially difficult to find. Perhaps the only ones you can find will be definitely *bad* eggs. Don't turn your nose up at these, as they can still be used.

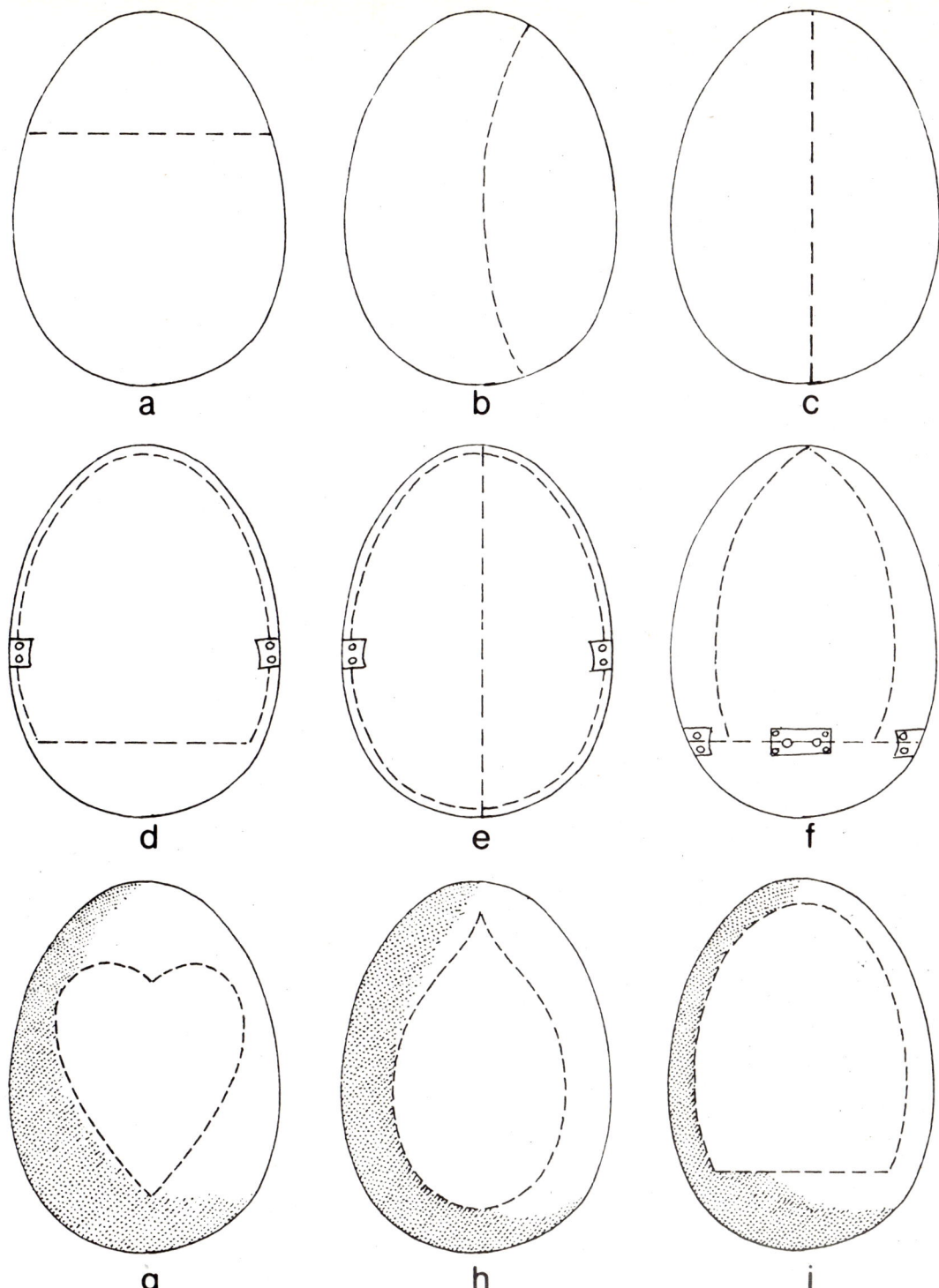

Cutting eggs: a) top cut; b) single door; c) half shell; d) double door; e) double door; f) petal cut; g) heart cut; h) helmet cut; i) alcove cut.

Whether an egg is good or bad can be determined by a simple test. An egg, newly laid, consists of a mass of yolk, together with what we call the white of the egg. Being heavier than water, these will cause the egg to sink when it is placed in water. But in an egg which has become rotten, the yolk and white have split up into other things, including gases. The gases escape from the shell, through the tiny pores that you can see if you examine an egg closely. The escape of gases makes the egg much lighter. Such an egg does not weigh as much as an equal amount of water does. If placed in water, it will not sink—it floats.

In short, a good egg sinks, but a bad egg floats.

A friend of mine keeps geese and gave me six eggs to work with when I began this book. Two of these eggs were not bad and when cut open the yolk stood up firmly and there was no odor whatever. I simply discarded the contents and handled the shells as outlined above. (When cutting spoiled eggs always make a hole at each end of the egg first, to prevent a vacuum buildup inside the shell.)

The remaining four were definitely *bad*—no doubt about it. After discarding the contents, as quickly as possible, I washed the shells under cold running water and pulled the membrane away from the egg and threw that away, too, for it was badly discolored and loosened. The shell underneath the membrane was also discolored but I knew that a paint job, glitter, or glass beads would hide this when I started decorating.

In the final analysis, by using a little planning, these eggs ended up just as attractively as the good eggs did.

Eventually I found several excellent sources of supply for goose eggs and also for the beautiful aqua-blue duck eggs (see appendix).

So now we have the egg contents emptied and the eggs as clean as we can get them. Before going any further, be sure the egg is completely dry. I like to let mine dry overnight.

If the egg you are working with is a goose egg with the membrane still intact it is a good idea to scrape this away where the hinge is to be glued (if this is not done the hinge and membrane may pull away from the shell).

When I am ready to glue the hinge, I take transparent Scotch tape and tape the cut sections of the egg together as closely as possible. Leave the small notch for the hinge open.

When you have only two pieces or halves as for a jewel box, this is easy. The double-door opening—very beautiful, but a little more tricky to achieve—should be left until you have had a little more practice. It is not at all hard to do once you master your cutting tool but takes a little more patience both to cut and to hinge.

To join two half shells, the hinge should be placed in the exact center. For the double-door opening, place it off center near the bottom. Use contact glue for the hinge, being very careful not to get any on the center pole of the hinge. (If you do, get it off at once with denatured alcohol.) Again, I allow plenty of time for the hinge to dry—several hours or overnight. I like to put a tiny bit of oil on the hinge again before decorating and wipe off any excess so trimmings will not be soiled.

What size hinge should you use? This depends on the egg size. A small, 1/2-inch hinge is about right for a chicken egg; 3/4-inch for a goose egg.

All of the goose eggs I have cut have had thick shells which did not break but duck and chicken eggs are a different story. These can also be cut nicely by using the Dremel, but it is advisable to coat them with gesso before cutting. This also goes for quail eggs, and even birds' eggs.

Yes, a few of my designs use bird eggs. No, I did not rob any nests (in most places this is illegal). Every spring I find a few eggs that have rolled out of the nests under the many big trees around our house and occasionally I find a few half shells from which the little birds have hatched. I always pick up these tiny eggs and save them. This year I found two robin egg half shells in that lovely shade called "robin egg blue" painted by nature herself.

And don't forget bantam eggs—if you can get these, buy them, for they, too, have their place in egg decoration. And the varicolored eggs of the Araucana chickens are very interesting. Avail yourself of eggs while they are in season, for they can be cut and stored for year-round decorating fun. The many different ways to go about decorating with eggs will be described in forthcoming chapters.

CHAPTER NINE

Eggs on the Half Shell

Angelfish Eggs

My husband, who has been highly amused all along by my ideas for egg decorations, suggested this one as a joke.

"You know," he said, sticking his head between the shower curtains and shouting above the noise of the running water, "these angelfish you've decorated the bathroom wall with look like eggs to me—eggs with fins—what can you make out of that?"

Right at the moment I couldn't think "what," but I was determined to think of something. I kept mulling it over all day and the next morning after he went to work I got busy.

To begin with, I selected a piece of heavy corrugated cardboard from a large box, cutting it approximately 14 × 17 inches. Don't try to make your picture too large; it must be in proportion to the size of the eggshells you are planning to use.

The cardboard was covered with a large sheet of white blotting paper glued down firmly with white glue and allowed to dry.

Next, I took a piece of pale blue satin (be sure to select a piece of good quality which is closely woven) and laid it over the blotting paper.

The satin had been previously ironed with a warm (never hot) iron so that it was perfectly smooth.

I cut the satin so that there was about a 2-inch extension around the cardboard on all sides, and pulled it as tightly as possible first over one edge and then another, to the back of the cardboard, securing it with masking tape so it would remain taut. Corners were folded back and taped down as I worked.

After this was finished, I had a very smooth surface for my egg picture.

Putting aside the background for the moment, I now started to prepare the eggs. I chose one large goose egg, carefully selected for size and shape, and one chicken egg.

I planned to use both pieces of the goose egg which was cut precisely in half after first drawing my guidelines with a pencil. The chicken egg was also cut exactly in half, but I used only one half.

When I am planning a picture I believe I can secure a better balance and a more pleasing effect by using uneven numbers—one bird, three fish, five butterflies, etc.

After the contents were removed and the eggs washed and dried, my three half shells were ready for the next step. They were laid on a piece of thin cardboard (the type the laundry puts in shirts) and a pencil line was drawn around each half so I would have the individual contour. The outline was then cut with a pair of sharp scissors.

I put contact glue around the edge of the cardboard and laid the half shell on it. (You may need to weight the shells down carefully until they are dry so they will make good contact with the cardboard.) If any cardboard edges extend after this operation, trim them off with your curved blade scissors.

Sometimes, due to a slight unevenness in the shell when cutting, you may have tiny unfilled spaces between the shell and the cardboard. Fill these in with glue, carefully wiping off any excess. Allow to dry.

Take white acrylic paint and, using a flat brush, such as Duro Art's No. 7 Red Sable bright, paint the entire surface of all three eggs as smoothly as possible. Allow to dry—this takes only a few minutes—and give them a second coat.

Be sure to wash your brushes carefully and thoroughly each time you use them, as the paint will dry quickly on these, too. After washing, shape the brush with your fingers and stand it on end in a glass or jar, brush end up.

Lay the three eggs on your blue satin background and trace around each egg with a pencil.

Remove the eggs. Again, using your pencil, draw the fins and tails of the angelfish. Draw graceful, curving lines for the seaweed—try to make it look as if it were moving by the action of the water and the swimming fish.

Draw a tiny shell or two clinging to the floating seaweed.

Using white acrylic paint on a fairly dry brush, fill in the outlines of the fins, tails, seaweed, shells, and tiny bubbles. Use your flat, ¼-inch brush to fill in the larger spaces. Tips of fins, tails, seaweed, and rising bubbles should be brushed in with either Grumbacher No. 1 or No. 2 brush.

When the paint on fins and tails is dry, cover the entire area with very light yellow. This may be acrylic white and yellow mixed, or white acrylic mixed with yellow water color.

Outline fins and tails with black acrylic paint, using No. 1 brush.

Using a crow quill pen and black India ink, draw the fine lines shown on the fins and tails, accentuating the heavier black areas as indicated with the No. 2 brush. Do not get ink on the silk at any time as it will blend into the silk. Draw with ink only on painted areas.

Paint seaweed green (white mixed with light green) shading with light brown and yellow to indicate shadows and sunlight reflected into the water. Mix the brown with white as these colors should be very delicate.

Outline the seaweed with black acrylic, using the No. 1 brush.

Paint the shells clinging to the seaweed in bright vermillion red and outline with black, making curving lines to shape the shells.

Go back now to the fins and add touches of light green and blue over some of the yellow areas. Add a touch of pale green to the bubbles and outline these with black acrylic, using the No. 1 brush.

Now we are going to paint the eggshells. That cardboard backing that we put on will make them easy to hold, and the white base coat will provide a good surface for the colors that are put on next.

Bear in mind that acrylic dries quickly, so do not try to paint too large an area at a time. Blend blue with white for the upper part of the fish, pink with white for the lower part. Blend the two together in the central part with pale yellow (white mixed with yellow). Try to make the blending smooth and without streaks. You might practice a little on a sheet of paper. Lots of times if I can't get the effect I want with a brush, I pat the paint with my fingers or a piece of soft cloth.

In fact I always paint with a piece of cloth in my left hand—it's a habit, I suppose—but I find it convenient for wiping brushes and cleaning them as I go along.

When you have these colors blended to your satisfaction and they are completely dry, you will be ready to put in the black markings.

First, draw these on lightly with a pencil; they are naturally somewhat irregular so you need not be exact. Do not get them too close together—the contrast of the black with the soft pastel colors is what makes the painting interesting.

Fill in the pencil lines with black acrylic paint and, using your crow quill pen, draw a few scales on the colored areas. These are just meant to be a suggestion of scales; you should not attempt to draw scales over the entire surface.

Draw the round eyes. These are circles of yellow outlined in black, with the inner circle orange and black, and the central black dot also outlined in yellow.

To make the side fins shown on the body of the fish look natural, draw them on with black and make a few white lines across the black area of the markings that shows through the fins. This gives them the look of transparency.

The gills are shown as narrow orange areas outlined with black, and a narrow band of orange is shown where the fins join the body.

After you finish painting the eggs glue them down into their outlines on the silk using contact glue, and the picture is complete. Be sure to sign it.

Eggs on a Velvet Band

These eggs on the half shell are very versatile, and especially pretty for a narrow wall space where a picture would not fit.

I like to start with a strip of cotton velvet or velveteen approximately 7 inches wide and about 26 inches long. Fold the velvet over and sew it together on the wrong side. Pull through to the right side and press down with your fingers. Sew a narrow seam on either edge of material—about ¼ inch from the edge.

Fold over at the bottom to form a point and sew. Attach a tassel of gold, white, silver, or dye a white tassel in Rit to harmonize or contrast with the velvet.

For my hanger at the top I used a discarded piston ring from a motorcycle. This was fitted with velvet which was sewn on the reverse side and pulled through to the right side by using a small safety pin. The velvet was then pushed on the piston ring and the end of my velvet strip was pushed through the velvet-coated ring and sewn to the back, tucking the rough edge under.

This decoration uses three chicken eggs. Select them for uniform size and shape and cut each egg exactly in half. It is a good idea to coat the

Eggs on velvet and leather bands.

shells with something to strengthen them before cutting. Gesso may be used, or enamel.

Lay each half shell on cardboard and draw around it with a pencil. As you work, number the shell and the cardboard.

Cut the cardboard, match it to each egg, and glue it firmly to the egg, using contact glue. When dry, trim any extending edges with sharp scissors and fill in any crevices with glue where contact between cardboard and shell is needed.

Each one of these eggs was given a background of a different color and when dry, the tropical butterflies were drawn on with black India Ink, using a crow quill pen.

The colors of the butterflies and flowers are not true to nature. They are done in the spirit of certain Chinese paintings which strive only for decorative effect. The Chinese will sometimes put flowers in a winter scene or place birds and butterflies on certain shrubs, trees, or flowers on which they do not normally feed, working out the combinations for purely aesthetic effect. Paint your butterflies and flowers as you wish so they harmonize or contrast effectively with the overall egg color and the velvet strip.

Using my crow quill pen and black ink, I drew the tendrils of vines on some of the eggs to enhance the feeling of lightness and grace.

After the eggs were completed and dry, I laid them on the velvet, spacing them about one inch apart. To do this easily, mark off an inch on a little square of cardboard and use it for spacing. It is easier than measuring with a large ruler each time.

Using contact glue, firmly affix the eggs to the velvet and let dry.

The tiny gold beads which frame each egg are metal and were bought by the yard in a department store. They are slightly heavier than gold pearl beads and also smaller in size and in better proportion to frame the eggs.

Another very effective idea for using a velvet or brocade hanging strip would be to reverse the eggs.

Spacing the eggs the necessary distance apart to be effective, glue a small plastic gold curtain ring to the velvet strip.

Make a cardboard backing for each egg as before, painting each egg with gold or silver Liquid Leaf.

Cut snapshots or family portraits to fit the flat cardboard to which the half shells have been glued. Edge the portraits with pearls, braid or metal trim.

Put glue on the curtain rings and place the curved part of the egg into place. Position each egg carefully so the line will be even.

Leather and "Horse Brasses"

The history of horse brasses make this particular decoration even more interesting. They were once amulets attached to the harnesses and were put on to insure good luck. Later they became simply a form of ornament.

Evidence of the number of designs varies between 1,000 and 1,800, and the older ones are much valued as antiques. This custom of ornamenting the horse brasses with pierced metal plaques is very old as some of the subjects, such as the crescent moon, indicate. They are usually circular in shape, with an upper pierced rectangular piece into which the strap was passed.

I have a number of these brasses, some of which are genuine antiques, others reproductions; all are interesting. Looking at them one day, I decided the designs would be attractive if painted on the half shell egg.

I started out with my usual method of cutting the eggs in half and gluing them to cardboard. I then drew the designs on the eggs, the crescent moon, wolf head, blazing sun, three feathers, cross and anchor. These were painted in two colors only, black acrylic and gold Liquid Leaf.

If you don't get your painting exactly right the first time, simply paint over it until it looks the way you want it to.

When you feel it is as good as you can make it, spray the finished egg with a protective coating and set it aside. Continue until the six designs you have decided upon are complete.

The background for these eggs is a strip of heavy saddle leather in a light tan shade which contrasts effectively with the black-and-gold painted "horse brasses." It is 26 inches long and about 2½ inches wide and I have tooled it by the same methods as described in the chapter on Western Eggs.

To do this, the eggs were placed on the leather and a line was drawn around each one with a lead pencil, placing them approximately one inch apart. After the design was stamped on the leather, the flat cardboard back of the eggs was glued into place.

Each egg was finished with a frame of the same metal beading as the "butterfly eggs." This design is thoroughly masculine and would look well in a den.

A Lavebo? You're Kidding!

Carl (my husband) was quite impressed with the way the "egg angelfish" picture turned out and took full credit for the idea. I couldn't argue; after all, he had suggested it.

But when I carried out the idea into other channels and made the two decorations I have just described, he began thinking again in terms of designing. He's good at it, so I try not to be envious.

Carl, whose uncle was Eugene Higgins, a well-known sculptor and painter, more or less grew up in his studio. Uncle Eugene's workroom was his haven and his refuge when, as a little boy, he was looking for a place to hide. When the old Contessa, his grandmother, was hunting through the house to mete out punishment for some childish prank, Uncle Eugene would hide the boy behind a pile of canvases until things quieted down.

Since these incidents occurred with almost clocklike regularity, Uncle Eugene often made the most of them by using Carl as a model. In such a situation it would have been almost impossible for Carl, who adored his uncle, not to absorb a goodly amount of artistic know-how.

Therefore, when my husband suggested, with a twinkle in his eye, that we make a goose egg lavabo I didn't protest overly much that it would be impossible. After my first reaction—"You've got to be kidding!"—I just sat still and listened.

The word "lavabo" has several meanings and, in its simplest sense, is merely a wash basin with its necessary fittings. The type we see most often nowadays are the very decorative ceramic representations of the real thing which was practical and functional and once widely used.

I have always liked the ceramic lavabos, considering them a graceful form of wall decoration, and have several on the walls of my home, one of which is antiqued in white and gold. It was this large one which suggested the idea of an "egg" lavabo to Carl.

Try, if possible, to choose a well-rounded egg as large as you can find; a big- double-yolk goose egg would be great. To have this design work out well, the egg should not be too pointed at the small end.

The egg I used was $3^{3}/_{4}$ inches long with a diameter of about $7^{1}/_{4}$ inches. If you are able to obtain a larger egg, do so, but size is really not important. The important thing is to choose materials and accessories which will be in proportion to the size of the egg you are working with.

For instance, the wooden plaque which formed the background is exactly right for this egg, being 7 inches high by 6 inches wide. The frame in which the plaque was placed was 17 × 15 inches and provided a perfectly sized background for it.

Using your drawing pencil, bisect the egg exactly in half.

Then, being careful to get your line straight, again bisect one of the halves lengthwise. This piece, when cut, will give you $^{1}/_{4}$ of the egg shell.

Cut the egg in half, using the Moto-Tool. Drain and wash. Cut the half shell where you have marked it. This will form the basin. Lay the half shell on a piece of cardboard and draw around it. Cut the cardboard and glue to the shell. Trim off any excess.

Lay the quarter shell on the cardboard. Cut to fit and glue edges. You

Egg lavabo, a graceful wall decoration.

now have a little basin open at the top. (Save the other piece for later use.)

When the glue is dry on both pieces, paint the exterior of both shells and the interior of the ¼-shell (and the cardboard backing which is exposed) with white enamel.

When the white paint is dry, give each shell two coats of white pearl lacquer or spray with Pearl Gold (this is a white pearl lacquer with a light golden shimmer). Light coats will avoid unsightly buildup.

Now glue your half shell in position on a small wooden plaque (you can find these in craft shops) which has been previously wood-stained to harmonize with the decor in whatever room this decoration is to be placed. Mine is stained in walnut.

It will be easiest if you ornament the half shell first before putting on the quarter shell which forms the basin.

Position two bands of narrow (⅛-inch), braided gold cord across the top—about one inch from the top—to suggest the cover. Place a strip of the same braid all around the edge of the egg where it is glued to the plaque.

The finial on the cover is the top of a purse-sized perfume flask glued into position and circled with 2-mm. white pearls.

The golden grape clusters were formed by sewing 3-mm. gold beads onto tiny scraps of yellow felt, bunching them up and overlapping the beads to give the effect of a graceful cluster, heavy at the top, just as they would appear in nature.

I used three of these clusters, a large one in the center, and two smaller bunches at each side. They were placed just below the gold cord which indicates the lid.

Between the clusters, I placed two gold-colored grape leaves, which had been part of an old charm bracelet. If you cannot find such leaves use heavy gold paper cut in the shape of a grape leaf.

This completed the upper part of the lavabo except for one small detail. I needed a spigot and I knew it would be impossible to find one small enough to be in proportion. Here husband Carl, who had been watching the proceedings all along, entered the picture again. He sat down and patiently carved a tiny spigot for me out of pecan wood and I painted it with gold Liquid Leaf and glued it on.

The upper part of the lavabo was now complete. (Note: if your husband isn't handy with a carving knife, try using, as I considered doing, a teardrop pearl to simulate a spigot.)

I was now ready to glue the basin in place. When dry, this was given two rows of the same gold braid across the rim and one row to frame the shell as before.

Three bunches of gold grapes, slightly smaller than the clusters used above, were now made up and placed on the basin. I did not repeat the gold leaves because they looked too heavy and out of proportion; instead, I joined the clusters with a loosely draped string of gold beads.

I completed the plaque by placing two gold keys, from the same charm bracelet as the grape leaves, on either side of my lavabo. The craft shops have tiny gold cupids of the right size which would be equally delightful—or for that matter, any other small ornament that suits your individual fancy. Just be sure it is in the right proportion to the design as a whole.

When this plaque was completed I was so enchanted with it that I wanted to give it added importance and eye appeal. And I did. It is the first thing people notice when they enter the room where it hangs on the wall. And, though the eggshell is not obscured and the shape is plainly seen, almost no one seems to recognize this fact at first—probably because it is so unusual and unexpected. I keep telling everybody that it really *is* an eggshell.

To frame it properly I hunted through a number of books on wallpaper patterns and finally selected a gold tone on tone paper with a very lightly raised, all-over design to use as a background. This was cut and glued to the cardboard.

I am always fascinated by antique picture frames and buy them whenever possible, repairing the plaster and repainting the frames when necessary, so I usually have several on hand from which to choose.

This frame, picked up at a garage sale, had been in very bad shape, but the basic design was beautiful and simple.

Part of the plaster had been broken off so I repaired this by mixing Durham's Rock Hard Water Putty with a small amount of water. Be sure to give this a very thick consistency. You can mold it with your fingers and press it on to the portions of the frame you are repairing, molding it lightly as you go. When the frame is painted or gold-leafed the repairs will not be noticeable, even if somewhat imperfectly made.

When the repairs to the plaster, which formed the inner decoration of the frame, were completely dry, I sanded the flat wooden part of the frame lightly, filled in some small holes and rough spots and let the filler dry.

When the filler had hardened sufficiently, it was sanded lightly so the surface would be even.

My next step—since wood is porous—was to coat the surface with a sealer. You may use shellac, acrylic or a sanding seal—it will work equally well. This is important because the sealer will fill up all the tiny pores in the wood and keep the paint, gold size, and varnish from being absorbed into the surface.

When this is dry, the entire surface should be painted with a red base coat. It has long been shown by experience that the best glow will be produced in the gold leaf if it has a red undercoating, so do not omit this step.

Follow the directions on the undercoating container; 30 minutes to an hour, depending on weather conditions, should be a sufficient drying time.

Now, using a soft brush, cover the entire surface of your frame, both wood and plaster (if you are working as I did with a frame that has both) with gold size, making your coat as thin as possible.

To do this you need not use an expensive brush; just be sure it is one that does not lose its hairs. If you find it easier and more convenient, you can spray the size on. (I like to spray it on because it is quicker and I don't have the small chore of cleaning the brush afterward.)

Let the gold size dry until it is tacky—this means semi-dry, but still a bit sticky to the touch. Try touching a tiny portion somewhere on the edge, for touching will deactivate the adhesive and the gold leaf will not stick.

When the gold size is ready, you can start the actual gold leafing process and I would advise you to do this in a room free from drafts, for the gold leaf is very, very thin and I found that even my own breathing disturbed it. (See chapter on colors, paints, and finishes for details on gold-leafing.)

But take your time, the gold size will not become deactivated (if it is not touched) for many hours and you can work as slowly and carefully as you like.

When I gold-leaf a frame or another flat surface, I like to take a small piece of cardboard, slide it under the leaf, leaving a bit on the edge hanging free.

Moving over to the portion of the frame I am working on, I place the overhanging bit on the gold size and then carefully and slowly slip the cardboard from underneath.

After I have placed all the larger pieces I usually fill in any spots where I need small pieces by placing the gold leaf with my fingers. A square of gold leaf may be torn or cut for this purpose.

For this particular project I wanted a really antique look, so I did not attempt to cover the frame entirely but left much of the base coat to show through.

As you lay the gold leaf down you will notice that it is wrinkled. Don't let this worry you. Take a piece of folded gauze and tamp all the gold leaf firmly on the flat surfaces. A brush may help you to get it into the cracks and crevices—be sure the brush is perfectly dry—and again use one that is of good quality and will not lose its hairs.

Continue working, pressing all the gold leaf into the gold size until your surface is reasonably smooth.

I like to let the frame dry for about 30 minutes at this stage and then burnish the surface with gauze. After this, I brush or spray on a good synthetic sealer to protect the surface and keep the gold leaf from dulling.

The frame completed, I was now ready to mount my wallpaper background within it.

This done and the cardboard securely tacked into place, I fitted a hanger to the back of the frame. Then I placed the lavabo plaque, measuring carefully so it would be equidistant, top, bottom, and sides, making tiny marks on the surface of the wallpaper so I would know exactly where to place the plaque after applying the glue to the back surface. I put contact glue on the back and my picture was now complete.

Before leaving this project, I would like to point out that the entire design was carried out in white and gold (with the exception of the wood-stained plaque, of course) and the simplicity of the color combination adds a great deal to its effectiveness. It can also be placed in almost any room in the house and will be in color harmony.

Though some of my designs do use a great deal of ornamentation—simulated and real jewels rather profusely—I think the simple ones are always the most effective. There is real danger, when working with something as small as an egg, in overdecoration. And, though at times I cover the egg up entirely with leather, cloth, or some other fabric, I never lose sight of the actual *shape* of the egg.

But Rococo, a style which flowered in France during the reign of Louis XV and spread to the rest of Europe, is fun, too. This style of art had its greatest influence during the 1700s; it was sophisticated, courtly, and elegant with gay charm and playfulness. It had movement, lightness, and grace even though great ornamentation was emphasized. It influenced painting, sculpture, architecture, furnishings, decoration and even costumes.

But for all its beauty, as time went on and it gradually became excessively decorated, it lost its popularity and simpler, less ornate styles became fashionable. There's a lesson here for us, just so much decorating and no more. Especially with eggs.

Actually this bit about overdecorating is something I have to keep telling myself because putting on trims is so much fun I am apt to get carried away.

Being in a generous mood, I gave Carl all the credit for the lavabo design and such modest success as we mutually achieved in working it out, but the next creation—if such it may be called—is entirely my own.

Baby in Bassinet

For this you will need:

  1 piece pink, blue, white, or yellow chiffon, about ½-yard long and 2½ inches wide.

  1 piece fine mesh, white nylon net—½-yard long by 2½ inches wide. Gather, leaving ¼-inch heading.

  1 piece fine mesh, white nylon net, about 6 inches long and 2½ inches wide.

  String of 2-mm. white pearls, 3½ inches long, approximately.

  ¼-yard white nylon lace, ½-inch wide.

  1 bunch velvet forget-me-nots in white or harmonizing color.

  2 1⅛-inch white plastic curtain rings.

  Plastic foam base, approximately 5¼ inches × 3¼ inches by ½-inch high.

  Bottle cap or cork (for base).

  Findings (pearls, braid, etc. for ornamenting tiny base).

  Contact glue, white thread.

  2 large duck or goose eggs. Directions are given for duck eggs.

If you use goose eggs make alterations as needed for supplies.
The eggs used were about 6 inches in diameter.

1. Spray-paint eggs (get Pekin duck eggs if at all possible) with pearl lacquer. Repeat three times, drying well between coats.

2. Pierce shell with corsage pin until space is large enough to insert curved blade scissors. (Moto-Tool may be used if you prefer.)

3. For bassinet you will need to cut away about 1/3 of the egg. If you are using scissors do not try to do this all at once. Cut away a small portion at a time, gradually rounding out and shaping the aperture until it is the size needed. Drawing the part to be cut out with a pencil first will give you a guideline.

4. In the same manner cut away almost, but not quite, half of the shell of another egg. This half-egg shell will be used for the hood. I like to leave on a bit of the curve.

5. Gather 6-inch-long nylon net for hood and glue to edge of shell. Use a clear glue as glue shows through.

6. Sew gathered lace to net.

7. Glue on pearl string where lace is sewed to net to cover stitches.

8. Glue hood egg firmly to bassinet egg, by slipping one inside the other and securing with contact glue. Let dry well.

9. Gather chiffon underskirt and glue firmly all around egg. The excess net of the hood is fluffed up a bit and pulled down so the underskirt will be placed over it, holding it in place.

10. Gather, with needle and thread, 1/2-yard-long nylon net overskirt and sew to chiffon.

11. Glue or sew forget-me-nots around edge of bassinet.

To elevate the bassinet slightly, it should be placed on a lid or cork to which a top and bottom curtain ring has been glued. This will show very little if at all, but someone is sure to look underneath so even this I like to ornament with braid and pearls for the sake of unity. Glue the stand to the base.

A tiny baby doll, dressed by banding it with narrow strips of the same color of chiffon used for the underskirt, adds a great deal to the effect. Small dolls may be bought at the dime store, craft shops, or ordered from Maid of Scandinavia.

This bassinet egg was "inspired" by a wooden cradle that has been in my family for over a hundred years. I was rocked in it when I was a baby and I also rocked my little son in it when he was small.

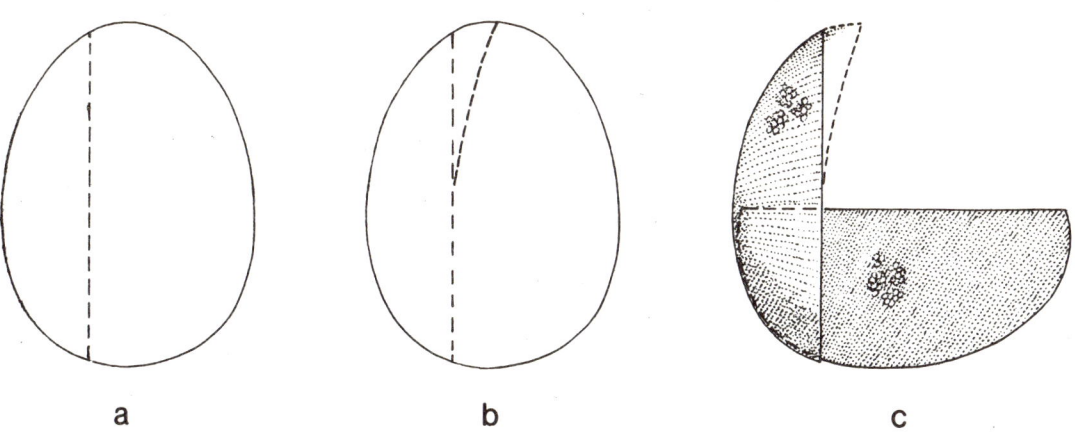

Making doll's bassinet: a) Cut duck egg for bottom; b) cut away not quite half of egg intended for hood; c) glue by slipping one egg inside the other.

Other suggestions for eggs on the half shell. Save your most attractive greeting cards, Christmas, Easter, Valentine, etc., especially those with tiny scenes.

Using the method described for family portraits, cut these to fit the flat cardboard to which the eggs have been glued, trimming as necessary. Give the pictures a protective coating and frame with an outline of braid or beading.

These can be placed on a narrow strip of cloth or leather as before or, by using an attractive background of cloth or paper, they can be framed as a series of small pictures—summer, winter, spring, autumn. Or use Oriental pictures, water scenes, or birds. Burlap, used as a background, or heavy decorator linen left in its natural color, are often very effective.

CHAPTER TEN

Colors, Paints, and Finishes

Color is what our eyes see when the light strikes them. When we look at grass, green light is reflected against our retina. The light reflected from a grape may be purple or blue, an apple red or yellow.

Different colors may affect us emotionally. Warm colors are exciting, cool colors quieting. The strength of the color also makes a difference. Pastels often have a lightness and grace, a springtime quality, which the deeper tones do not. Deep tones may have the richness and jewel-like color of a stained glass window.

Since decorating eggs and decorating *with* eggs is a craft now practiced by many as a year-round hobby, some discussion of color may be helpful.

Most eggs, compared to other objects in a room, are relatively small, yet they can be used most effectively as color accents. They can even, by judicious combination with other materials, be a dominant note.

An egg is something you can "dress up or dress down." Trimmed with braid and pearls and placed on an attractive stand, it can add a note of opulence to your most elegant room with a style that is distinctive and different. You can make eggs into clever little jewel boxes or incense holders—so beautiful they are almost jewels in themselves.

Yet eggs are versatile; they can be covered with cotton prints or gingham and used in the kitchen or in some other informal room for a bright and cheerful note.

Eggs need not always be covered or painted. Sometimes the shell is so beautiful and translucent that it needs very little trim and should be left in its natural color. Swan eggs, aqua-blue duck eggs, turkey eggs, Araucana chicken eggs, and guinea eggs all have interesting colors, spots, or speckles of their very own. Even the brown eggs laid by certain breeds of chickens are lovely without any additional coloring.

Many of these eggs, if the shells are clean and unmarred, can be used just as they are. They can also be cut for single or double doors, made into window or alcove eggs, trimmed sparingly with braid, pearls, simulated or real jewels and become extremely attractive.

Even the shells most often used, those large white chicken eggs found in every grocery store, can be carefully selected for size and quality.

Some of the eggs mentioned may be obtained only at certain seasons of the year. If this is so, buy them when available, cut, tape, and store them safely. This will make it possible for you to have the pleasure of year-round decorating whenever your time permits.

But for imperfect eggs and eggs that may be soiled to the point where washing has little effect, painting or covering in some manner is the best possible answer. The egg can still be used.

Today's markets offer so many different types of paint and color possibilities that it is a real joy to consider the choices.

I particularly like the acrylics because they are so quick-drying and easy to use. It is also possible to paint over a mistake—even putting white over black if necessary.

A set of the small tubes is inexpensive and will give you the basic colors which mix well. However, I like to use a great many different shades and variations of shades and for many of my decoration ideas I like to mix water colors with acrylic to obtain the exact color I want.

This is very easy to do. Place a very small amount of tube water color (I prefer the Grumbacher water colors as they are very clear and free from muddiness) on a glass or china plate. Near this, place the white acrylic. Gradually add the color into the white until you have the shade you need.

Acrylic paint may be thinned with water to make a very pale shade, particularly useful when painting a large area such as an egg for one of the eggheads. A flesh tint can be made by mixing pink with white, yellow with white, brown with white, or even orange with white. This mixture usually needs to be slightly thinned. Be careful to add only a drop at a time until the desired consistency is reached.

Acrylic paint is odorless and easy to handle. It will wash readily before it has completely dried but when dry is almost impossible to remove. If you have made a mistake—paint over it. Be sure to clean your brushes carefully each time you use them, because the paint will quickly harden on these, too.

It is also possible to obtain many soft shades of color by mixing colored India inks with the white acrylic paint. I use India ink in all shades, but especially black and dark brown for drawing on the eggs. For this, use a very fine camel-hair brush or a crow quill pen. Do this only after the paint is completely dry, otherwise it will scrape off and collect on the pen point.

As mentioned in a previous chapter, I frequently use a very nearly transparent pearl lacquer as a protective finish for decorated eggs.

For a hard, brilliant gloss finish I find I get very good results with a celluloid enamel which is used as a finish for fishing lures. (This may be purchased in convenient one-ounce bottles.) I particularly like this enamel as it is waterproof. Inevitably the time comes when an egg, used in a room as a bit of decoration, must be dusted or cleaned in some manner. Eggs painted with this enamel can simply be wiped off with a damp cloth.

The white enamel of this group, which comes in seven different shades, also serves as a base for a luminous paint made by the same company. Luminous paint will provide some exceedingly beautiful and unusual effects. But a word of caution: this paint should be kept out of the reach of children; it is only for adult craftsmen. There is no danger in using it provided the manufacturer's instructions, clearly set out on the label, are followed. When I use this paint, I always do so out of doors or in a well-ventilated room. If I plan to do several eggs, I wear plastic gloves.

Luminous paint was developed to be used on lures for which it is especially effective in early morning, evening, and at night. In using it on the eggs or figures to be placed inside the eggs, it should be applied over a well-dried base coat of clear or white celluloid enamel for best results. You can apply it over the entire egg or figure, or it can be applied to the eggshell in stripes and dots.

This paint comes in white, mayfly green, special yellow and firefly blue. I have been completely fascinated with this paint which will pick up light from either sunlight or artificial light and glow softly in the dark after the lights are turned out.

I have used this paint in decorating eggs in a variety of ways such as drawing flowers with India ink on white eggs and filling them in with one of the luminous colors so the flowers will shine in the dark. Eggs like these may be either hung from a tree or placed in a bowl.

Window eggs, in which the figure stands out, are delightful. For these, I went to the toy department and found a number of miniature farm animals and other figures—Ferdinand the Bull, Billy Whiskers, a horse, rooster, rabbit, and a little boy.

After the egg was cut so the figure would be well revealed, I edged it with ribbon or straw braid, and put a small platform of plaster of Paris in the bottom for the figure to stand on. If the egg was to be hung, I put on a bell-cap hanger, using monofilament fish line, nearly invisible from a slight distance, further to enhance the unusual effect.

After the figures were painted white and well dried, I repainted several in each of the luminous colors and put them in the eggs. After the lights are turned out they appear to be suspended in the air. You can add to the strange effect by giving the interior of the egg a coat of white glue and applying white crystals.

Another very effective idea is to coat the egg with Herter's French Flitters. This is a finish that reflects light far more than does any other known type and it is also a lovely translucent finish. These flitters which are tiny, round, hard reflectors are of the type used for coating outdoor signs at night so that when lights are put on them they flash clearly. They pick up and reflect light from every possible angle.

Flitters are very easy to use. Apply a coat of adhesive (Clear Flitter adhesive) and allow this to dry until it becomes tacky. An ordinary salt shaker works well for sprinkling the flitters. When dry, shake out the excess and put it back for future use.

Flitter adhesives are obtainable in transparent, black, white, red, yellow, and blue. These flitters, used over an egg which has been decorated by painting, will give it a very rich appearance and at the same time soften the colors.

Most of us are familiar with the metallic glitter sold in craft shops and dime stores and these will serve to decorate eggs if given a protective finish. But if you want metallics that are both beautiful and lasting, I would recommend Herter's Swiss Metallics.

These are tiny bits of special, hard, nonwater-absorbing material, .004 of an inch thick. They do not change color on top of or beneath transparent finishes. After putting on the adhesive with a brush, let it dry slightly. Again, using a common salt shaker, sprinkle on the metallics which come in either gold or silver.

Egg crafting is a very rewarding hobby and for your finest creations try to obtain materials which will withstand the test of time, for it is very disheartening to see something you have put a lot of work into start to tarnish.

With this in mind I always try to select nontarnishable trims. But how are you going to tell? Will the gold braid of today be as bright tomorrow? Buying quality materials is only part of the answer for unexpected small tragedies will still occasionally occur to our most cherished keepsakes. The best answer I have been able to come up with is—whenever possible—put on a protective finish.

The easiest way to do this is to put on a clear coat of fixative. There are several fixatives that will give you either a glossy, shiny finish or a dull matte finish. Grumbacher's Hyplar matte medium and varnish (Cat. No. 528-4) will give a nice satin finish with a very low gloss. Or you may use a clear plastic spray for high gloss results. Even clear fingernail polish, slightly thinned with acetone, may be used and applied with a brush.

Be sure to put your protective finish over the braid before putting on any jewels for otherwise these will dull. For the velvet-covered alcove or window eggs I spray the gold or silver cord or braid with a light coat before I put it on the egg.

It is a good idea to protect metallic paints, metallic sequins, or gold and silver papers with a coat of clear finish. Spray the eggs covered with velvet or other fabrics with a protective cloth finish—Scotchguard is a good preservative for fabric.

Enamel and metallic spray paints are so easy to use that you can quickly make enough eggs for a Christmas tree or Easter decoration by spraying them all at one time, making five of each color, on a simple, easy-to-make drying rack.

All you need is empty egg cartons, plaster of Paris, and some long finishing nails. Cut off the top and closing flap of the carton and turn the carton over. Press the nails up through each one of the little depressions.

Mix plaster of Paris. Suspend the carton with the nails hanging down between two fruit jars. Fill the depressions with the plaster. Adjust nails so they will hang straight down and harden. The plaster adds weight so the carton will not tip easily when the eggs are hung on the nails. Cover the carton with aluminum foil, letting the nails stick through so the spray paints will not melt the carton material. These cartons are so inexpensive that they can be discarded after use.

A more permanent type of rack may be made for drying chicken eggs by driving long finishing nails through a board, spacing them two to three inches apart. Slip the eggs over the nail and allow to hang until dry. For goose eggs, use longer nails and space them three or four inches apart. I prefer to use narrow boards and place only one row of eggs on each.

Antique finishes, either for window eggs or eggs left whole, can be very effective, especially over metallics.

To gold-leaf an egg, glue on a bell cap to which a piece of narrow braid or velvet ribbon has been attached to serve as a hanger.

Paint the egg a rich, deep color, using dark blue, green, red, or even brown or black—a deep orange can be striking. Allow to dry completely.

Holding the egg by the hanger, paint or spray on gold-leaf adhesive. Follow directions on adhesive container, waiting 30 minutes, or until adhesive becomes tacky, ("tacky" means partially dry, with the surface still slightly sticky to the touch).

Suspend the egg while drying and do not touch it with your fingers as this will inactivate the adhesive and the gold-leaf will not adhere.

When drying time is complete, hold the egg by the hanger and place it on a piece of gold-leaf, gently rolling the leaf around the egg. Place additional leaf as needed on the egg. The egg may be completely covered or some of the base color may be allowed to show through, adding to the antique look.

Brush off any excess leaf. I like to use a 3/8-inch Grumbacher brush for this purpose. The brush may also be used for applying small pieces of leaf.

For antiquing, mix a water-based color such as casein (Deep Flex makes a good one) to a thin consistency. Any color can be used; grays, tans and browns all give good results.

Paint the entire surface with the color. Any type of brush will do, but, as always, a good one that will not lose hairs will save time and work.

Allow the color to dry for 15 to 20 minues (depending to some extent on weather conditions when you are working).

Using a damp, soft rag, wipe off but do not try to remove entirely. If some areas become too light you can repeat the process.

When you are satisfied with the results, let the egg dry a little longer and then polish lightly with a soft, dry cloth.

Brush or spray on gold-leaf sealer. Let dry.

Now, if you plan to put on gold braid trim, either prepaint the trim with a protective coating or glue it to the egg and then again spray the entire egg with a protective coat.

After this trim is in place, rhinestones should be put on last.

Now, for a few pointers about the gold-leaf itself. Gold-leaf of the finest quality is called "Wind Gold" or "XX Deep Patent Gold Leaf." This gold-leaf comes between sheets of tissue. The tissue backing makes this type much easier to handle than regular gold-leaf. It can even be cut in small pieces with scissors by carefully cutting through both tissue and leaf.

Always try to work with gold-leaf on a dry day and do so in a room where there is no air draft. Gold-leaf may also be placed on a small sheet of cardboard and slipped off on to the object you are working on.

If you are gold-leafing a stand for the egg, you will need to use your brush for transferring small pieces of leaf into cracks and crevices. Don't worry too much about covering the stand entirely—again, it will add to the antique look if some of the base coat shows through.

Don't overlook the artistic possibilities of silver leaf—which is really aluminum. Because it is aluminum instead of silver it will not tarnish. These leaves measure $5\frac{1}{2} \times 5\frac{1}{2}$ inches and are often used where the effect of silver is desired. Real silver leaf is purer than sterling, but if used any place except on glass where it is possible to back it up and protect it from the air, it will tarnish in a very brief time, so it is not very practical for egg decoration.

Some interesting finishes with metallics can be obtained by using Rub 'n Buff. Paint eggs black, deep blue, red, brown, or any rich, dark color. Let dry. Apply Rub 'n Buff unevenly for an antique look.

Some of the most beautiful metallic effects are achieved with copper paint either left "as is" or antiqued, and I have often wondered why this finish is not more often used.

Lacquer finishes of the type used for model airplanes finish eggs nicely and have the added advantage of coming in many colors and small sizes. If you feel, as I do, that you do not want to decorate too many eggs in one color you will enjoy the fun of trying out the different shades.

Of course, if you are decorating many eggs for a large project such as church, school, or community Christmas trees, you may decorate a number of eggs by painting them the same color, mixing the colors when the eggs are hung.

When you paint with lacquer, apply the paint always by brushing in the same direction, either vertically or horizontally. Several light coats will give a more pleasing effect than one heavy one.

Work slowly, allowing plenty of drying time between each coat. Try not to let the lacquer build up as additional coats are added. Stir your paint frequently as you work. Clean your brushes carefully each time they are used.

No book on egg decoration is really complete without at least touching on the Ukrainian method called Pysanka. The name means literally "to write."

This art of decorating Easter eggs has been practiced in the Ukraine for centuries and has been handed down from one generation to another. Many of these eggs are masterpieces with great detail, featuring many layers of colors applied in designs, usually geometrically exact.

Actually the method is similar to that of batik, for the melted wax, when applied to planned spaces on the egg protects it from the dye. The various colors are put on successively by repeated waxing and dyeing, starting with the lightest shade of color first.

You will need cold dyes and preferably beeswax. For brushes, I use No. 1 and No. 2 camel-hair brushes to make the fine lines. Traditionally, an instrument called a kistka is used for this type of egg decoration and if you are interested in taking it up seriously and doing the more intricate designs it would be well to invest in one.

If you want to decorate the eggs in simple forms (and they are meant to be eaten), be sure to use colors such as Cakolor which will be safe for eating.

If you want to decorate them for keeps, blow out the eggs and dip them in any rich-colored, nonedible dye of your choosing. You may even make this yourself by using crepe paper, a small amount of water and a tablespoon or so of vinegar to set the color.

Try to get large, clean, white eggs, preferably chicken eggs which seem to give the best results. Don't wash them unless absolutely necessary, and then do so only in plain water. If the natural oils are removed from the shell of the egg the dye job will not be even.

Your wax should always be quite hot, preferably melted in a double boiler. Using a brush, apply the wax to the warm egg (it will dry too quickly on cold eggs and will not flow evenly). In warm weather I find bringing the eggs to room temperature is all that is necessary, but in cold weather the eggs should actually be warmed by some means before you start to work on them.

If you have not made these eggs before, you may need to practice a little before you can achieve the intricate designs. Starting with the lightest color, dip the egg into the dye bath. If you plan to have several colors, repeat waxing and dyeing with the next lightest color. Be sure to rinse the eggs in cool water after each dye bath and dry them before rewaxing.

When dyeing is completed, gently clean the wax from the finished egg with a solvent, such as denatured alcohol. This will leave a very light gloss. If you want a high shine, shellac, thinned with alcohol and applied with a lint-free cloth, may be applied. Rub the solution over the egg quickly and gently. Set aside for drying.

Maid of Scandinavia list a Ukrainian Easter Egg kit (No. 81086) in their catalog which includes a booklet showing the traditional designs. The kit contains six packages of coloring material, special wax for designs, designing tool and a folder explaining the meaning of the eggs and their designs.

While I find the Ukrainian eggs interesting and beautiful, I have always been more fascinated by the rush-pith eggs made in western Poland. These eggs use wool applique which is quite different from other types of egg decoration, in intricate designs.

Moravians decorate eggs like this to make toys for young children, putting pebbles inside to make them rattle. Sometimes these eggs are kept suspended all year from the ceiling and an Easter dove with pith decorations may be suspended over the cradle. Once, long ago, rattles were thought to keep away evil spirits—it is only in recent centuries that they have become mere toys.

It was even believed at one time that the rush pith served some magical protective purpose and it was believed that the reeds had to be picked at the time of the full moon, when they were supposed to contain the pith, and to be empty when the moon waned.

I am told that rush pith, which is called binsa, grows in Pennsylvania, is easy to find at Easter time. The approved method of getting it out of the rushes is by pushing it out with a matchstick. Its natural color is usually white or pale yellow, and though some people practice staining it with water colors, it is usually left unchanged.

There seem to be as many ways of decorating eggs as there are people interested in putting on the decorations. In some sections of Europe straw-covered eggs are made. Tubes of barley straw are soaked in water and the tubes cut lengthwise. This forms a flattened surface which is cut into different shapes and these are applied to the shells.

To me, all of this adds up to the simple fact that wherever you happen to be in the world, if you want to decorate eggs, you use what is available. In my section of the country I would find it difficult to obtain barley straw and rush pith is altogether unavailable.

I looked around last spring and considered what I might have. What I had most of was Johnson grass—just plain old Johnson grass. Sometimes this is useful for feeding cattle, but it is a pest in my garden if there ever was one, with roots that dig down deep and are practically impossible to eradicate.

Surely, I thought, it couldn't be all bad—and wouldn't it be fun to use it in some manner for a new style of egg decoration?

To start, I enameled several eggs in brilliant colors which also served the purpose of strengthening the thin shell of the egg.

The head of this grass consists of branches like a little Christmas tree, each branch bearing many seeds. Just below the head is solid stem about 1/8 of an inch thick. I cut off the head and cut a number of these straight stems. They can be dried in silica sand or simply set upright in a jar or bottle and allowed to dry naturally.

The usable part of the stem is about 12 to 14 inches long. When this was dry I gave each stem a coating of white enamel. After the enamel dried, I cut the stems into 1/2-inch pieces and used them to make a very attractive lattice-work decoration on the eggs.

If you want to make these eggs even more interesting, before cutting the stems, coat the white enamel with luminous paint. The latticework will then shine in the dark after the lights in the room have been turned off.

If you don't happen to have Johnson Grass in your section of the country, maybe you've got something even more interesting and decorative—right in your own backyard—if you will just let your imagination play with the idea of using all sorts of unusual materials.

There are so many different types of paints, finishes, and protective coatings on the market that it would be impossible to list each one of them and their particular qualities. I would suggest that before you buy a preparation you read the directions carefully. If you are still uncertain as to what the results will be, experiment before using. Glossy decoupage spray may be used over white glue or waterbase paint like acrylics with beautiful results, but it will soften enamels and cause them to run.

On the other hand, enamels which have a high gloss—many of them are waterproof—do not need a protective finish. Braid trims applied to these may be sprayed before placing on the egg.

New paints and finishes are constantly being introduced and experimenting with them for those of us who are dedicated eggers can add a lot of excitement and pleasure to our particular craft.

CHAPTER ELEVEN

Make Your Own Egg Stands

For your finest creations you will probably want to buy some of the exquisite egg stands readily available. These will quickly give you a beautiful effect—with no effort on your part. I recommend them highly since most of the stands you make yourself cannot equal their beauty, but making your own can be more fun.

And the fun of doing your own is, I believe, what most of us happy crafters are interested in learning about. As we have gone through the various chapters of this book I have described a number of stands in detail, along with the method used for decorating the eggs.

Eggs and their stands should be considered in relation to each other; style, size, and materials should all be coordinated into a pleasing whole. Color, especially, should be carefully thought out and, as you have probably noticed, many of the velvet-covered eggs have had the velvet, or the color of the velvet, repeated in the stand on which the egg was placed.

Almost always, except in the Leather-Clad Westerners, I have used only two colors in decorating the individual egg, and sometimes just one, accenting the color with gold, white, or silver braid and pearls. Of course, there are exceptions to every rule, but generally speaking, a hodgepodge of colors is very seldom as effective as the simplicity of one or two.

Jars and bottles placed in silica sand in the hot sun take on opalescent colors.

Egg stands can be made out of just about anything. They can be built with cardboard and then painted and trimmed to look like metal. They can be made with metal caps from aerosol bottles, caps or lids of the flat-screw type, ball bearings, lock nuts (from electrical supply stores), large nuts of all types, knobs, drawer pulls, spools, curtain rings, either singly or in stacks, and even small candleholders.

Some of the loveliest and simplest stands can be fashioned out of large pearl beads, the silver or gold rose-shaped beads (available in craft stores), and large wooden beads.

All of these will work well and be effective but, since I love antiques and the antique look even in eggs and egg stands, there is another way of making stands that I would like to talk about.

You have probably observed that I frequently combine small glass bottles with other materials to make stands. Save all your little perfume bottles. Look for small glass toothpick holders or any other small, pleasingly shaped container made of glass that takes your fancy. When you have a little collection, gather them all up, prepare to give them the antique look, and have fun watching it happen.

Find a couple of shallow wooden boxes; the flats that plants are sold in are fine, being just about the right height. If you can't get these maybe your friendly neighborhood grocer will save you a couple of wooden apple boxes.

Even the foil containers that frozen baked goods come in can be used if you put a few drain holes in the bottoms. Just about anything, except cardboard which will disintegrate when wet, can be used, but be sure to make drain holes.

You will need more of the same silica sand that you used for drying flowers. If you have some of this sand left, use it. If you are no longer using the sand to dry flowers, strain it to get out the bits of leaves and petals and use it again for this project.

If your boxes are not completely solid, line them with old newspapers before pouring in the sand which should be spread in the container to a depth of one or two inches.

Now, take your little bottles and place them on the sand, a couple of inches apart. The small toothpick holders, etc. go in also. If you want to antique some larger pieces of glassware at the same time go ahead. Just don't crowd the articles; each should have its own little territory.

Try to put your little box or boxes in a protected spot where children or animals will not overturn or disturb it, but not in a spot protected from the sun, for it is the hot, blazing, summer sun that is going to be the prime factor in doing the work for you.

Collectors of bottles and old glassware often prize even the broken bits picked up in desert areas where the combined action of sun and sand have turned these into a lovely amethyst, green, or yellow, sometimes, even an iridescent rainbow of colors.

That is exactly what we are planning to do with our sun, sand, and bottle arrangement. If it is easily accessible, I would suggest that you place your box on the top of the garage or some other place where it will receive as many hours of sunshine during the day as possible and, of course, summer, when the sun is warmest, is the best time of the year.

Day after day the sun will be on the job, working for you to impart color to your bottles and make them far more interesting than if they were colorless. Part of the fun is the fact that there is just no way to be certain what color you are going to come up with.

To my way of thinking, lavender is the loveliest and I am always delighted when my glassware turns this faint, clear purple. But I'm happy if I get green or yellow; even happier if I get blue. Occasionally I am disappointed—I get nothing at all. Some glassware simply refuses to color no matter how long it is left out in the sun. If this happens, I simply take it away or, if I especially like the piece, use it as is.

If you live, as I do, in a Western area where the sun blazes down day after day—we often have temperatures over 100 degrees for 10 or 15 days in a row—you will notice your glassware starting to turn in just a few weeks. I have a piece out right now that shows a faint amethyst tinge after just one week.

The average time for a piece to turn is about three weeks but, if you live farther north, it may take a little longer. If it rains, be sure to empty any open containers as soon as possible to prevent ugly stains from forming on the glass.

Though the colors I have mentioned above are the most common, you can get almost any shade by sunning a sufficient number of bottles. The reason for this is that the particular components that are combined to make the glass determine what color that piece of glass will turn. Since different pieces of glassware are made from different components, you get a variety of colors when you sun a variety of glass items.

When your little containers have deepened in color you can use them for stands in any way that suits your fancy. Place them on lids for a wider base; paint the lid or cover it with velvet or braid. Add a band of braid around the tops of bottles if they had a screw-on cap. Put a curtain ring at the top for the egg to rest in; color or cover it if necessary for a pleasing effect.

Egg stands, though most often used (with the possible exception of hangers), are just one means of displaying eggs attractively.

For eggs that are fashioned to hang from a Christmas tree, bare branch egg tree, from a doorway, or other place, there are a number of attractive ideas and materials for both the top and bottom and even the sides of the eggs.

Hangers of the simple Christmas tree type are often used. Ribbon—silk or velvet; cord—gold or silver; and monofilament fishing line, nearly invisible from a distance, are other suggestions. Broken gold chains or chains cut from inexpensive costume jewelry give added richness to jeweled eggs. Bell caps of all types and sizes are available for the top of the egg; they may be simple or very ornate.

The sides of jeweled eggs, meant to glitter and catch the light from every angle, may be draped with pearls, beads, or tassels.

For the finial at the bottom of the egg, I sometimes really let myself go and make them long and fancy, using pendants from discarded earrings or necklaces. Bracelets, too, can often be cut or pried apart and bits of jewelry used from these to make exquisite decorations. Use gold, white or silver tassels. Dye the white tassels in a matching color with Rit.

Frame your eggs in sets or series just as you would a picture of an antique collection of interesting small objects. Paint or gold-leaf the frame, or leave it in a natural wood tone. Mat with cloth or wallpaper—even plain brown wrapping paper can be painted or treated and can be used attractively as a background material—have it either perfectly smooth or intentionally heavily crumpled for an interesting texture.

Wooden peg board can be used to display a collection of eggs. Framed plywood, stained, can serve as a background. Use a large piece of leather—it may even be more interesting if it is somewhat irregular in shape.

A long strip of leather, placed horizontally or vertically, tooled or left plain, can be used.

An egg on which the decoration has been carried out in a very unusual manner may be displayed in a glass case. If you can't get the glass start looking for a clear lucite box.

I come from a long line of bottle, string, and paper-sack savers. The boxes in which I put things away are stored where I can readily put my hand on small items that I don't want to lose among the larger articles.

While I realize this pack-rat tendency can get cumbersome at times, I try not to let it, maintaining some sort of order which I often refer to as "logical confusion." I try to keep more or less related objects together and label them—bottles, velvet scraps, braid, jewelry findings, etc.—and I find this saves me hours of searching time. Luckily, I live in a house with an upstairs largely unused since my children have grown up and married, so I have a good place to put my craft items when they are not in actual use.

Far be it from someone who acts as helter-skelter as I do to urge others to develop habits of neatness, but I must admit, no matter how unwillingly, that in the long run taking time to put things away and labeling will save many hours of frustrated hunting when you need a particular item and can't remember where it is.

With this idea in mind, keep materials for possible use as stands or other means of displaying the eggs in a separate place of their own.

In the summer, when other activities keep you busy, put out a box or two of small bottles and containers and let the sun turn them into soft, lovely colors. Put them away and when winter comes they will be all ready for many happy hours of picking and choosing just the right one for that very special egg you plan to decorate for yourself, as a gift to a friend, or even for sale.

CHAPTER TWELVE

Eggs That Bloom in the Spring

It's not very often that a crafty idea comes into my head while I am cooking breakfast—I'm usually too sleepy—but one morning last spring this happened rather naturally.

Stumbling around, I inadvertently cracked an egg on the rim of the skillet, and, instead of hitting it squarely in the middle as I usually do, I missed and simply broke off a piece at one end. The yolk and white slipped out neatly. I stared at the shell and decided in some surprise that what I was holding resembled a little basket. Why hadn't I thought of this before?

I washed the shell and put it on the drainboard, upturning it to dry. Then, using my curved blade scissors while the shell was still moist, I trimmed the edge a little more so that it would be even.

I find that eggs will cut more easily right after the contents are discarded, but you can try spraying the shells with a hardening agent and cutting to size later if you prefer.

At the time I knew I was going to make something out of the egg, but I was not sure *what*. While my mind wrestled with possibilities, I sprayed the interior with a coat of instant finish decoupage. I knew this would go a long way toward preserving the firmness of the delicate eggshell whatever it ultimately turned out to be.

What I wanted to make was a decoration that was dainty, not too elaborate, and springtime fresh. No more beads and sequins, this egg was going to dare to be different.

Since I'd been busy sewing some housedresses for myself I guess my mind was on cloth and I decided to try out something simple with some of the leftover cotton print scraps. So, after several trial-and-error attempts, I cut four rounded triangular pieces. Using white glue, I proceeded to apply these to my little egg basket.

The job when finished didn't quite please me, it looked bunchy and clumsy. So I tried again (by now I had saved up several more eggshells) and this time I cut three ¼-inch slashes along the upper side of the triangle and two slashes of the same size on either side of the triangle.

After applying white glue to the underside of the cloth (you will need four pieces for each egg), I pressed down the upper part of the triangle first, flipping it over the rim of the egg and firming it down. If your cloth absorbs the glue, add more as needed.

I now started pressing the cloth over the rest of the egg, tucking the tiny slashed pieces over each other for a smooth fit. This worked fine and I put on the other three quarters the same way, overlapping each one a little so no part of the egg would show. Since eggs vary, it is impossible to cut a pattern that will be an exact fit but it is better to get it a little too large than too small. The eggs I used were approximately 3¾ inches in diameter.

Also, when you are covering the eggs this way, it is best to work on one quarter of each egg at a time, letting it dry before you go on to the next one. Smooth each piece as you go along and the result will be a neat fit. Cut an extra slash here and there if necessary or cut the slash a little deeper. Trim off any extra cloth with sharp scissors.

I'd like to note here that I tried a number of other materials for covering eggs in this manner and some of them such as the gingham checks also worked fine, as did small polka dots, and even some thin silks were very attractive.

However, for what I had now decided these eggs were going to be used, I liked the flowered, fairly thin cotton materials best. The next time I shopped, I hunted for bright gay cloth with a small all-over flower design that seemed right for my purpose. One-fourth yard will cover four shells of this basket type.

Since I planned to use these eggs in different ways, I bought several yards of pastel ribbon, which I cut into approximately half-yard lengths, and tied a small bow in the center of each. These were then put aside.

I also bought some white braid (rickrack would be fine also) which I

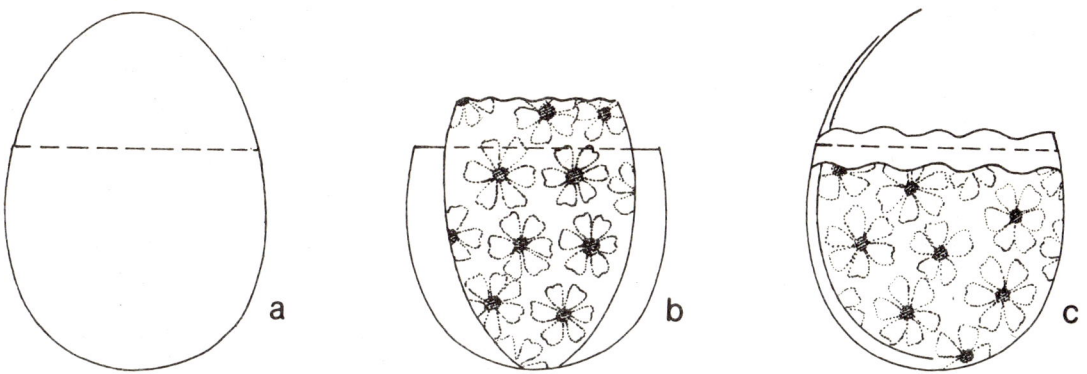

Egg baskets and candleholders: a) Cut away about one-third of shell; b) cover each section and flip cloth over rim; c) Let braid extend about 1/8-inch upward.

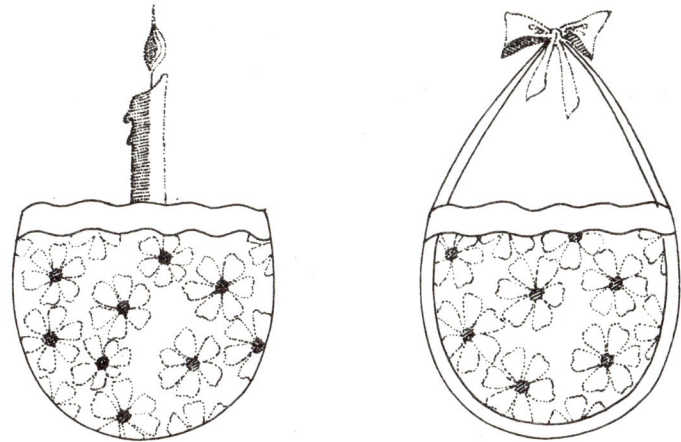

used around the rims of the eggs to give the illusion of flower petals and further enhance the tulip shape.

This was glued around the outer rim of the shell extending upward about 1/4 of an inch and left to dry for a few minutes.

Then I sprayed the shells again both inside and out with two coats of decoupage spray.

After the spray was dry, I glued a 7/8-inch white plastic curtain ring to the inside bottom of each egg. (This may be done before spraying if you prefer; it really does not matter.) These rings are washable and will not warp out of shape under heat.

Be sure to get this type of curtain ring because we are now making candleholders. To set the candles I heated paraffin to the just warm stage—melted and pourable. (Never let your paraffin get too hot for it will burn.)

Country Cousin eggs, used as candleholders, circle a centerpiece of flowers.

I poured a small quantity in each egg and let it cool slightly, then positioned a 3½-inch candle in each curtain ring. You can use any type candle in these holders, but this spiral twist type is about the right size to look well in proportion to the holders. They come in pastel colors and I bought them at the dime store.

I turned my attention to my other set of covered baskets, picking up the ribbons I had tied into little bows.

The two loose ends of the ribbons were glued vertically around the eggs to make little handles, clipping off any excess after about a ½-inch overlap was formed on the bottom.

After the handles dried, I measured the amount of braid needed for each individual egg, cut and glued it firmly around the upper edge, again letting the little scallops project upward about ⅛-inch.

These tiny baskets were hung for display on a wire rack used for water glasses and filled with jelly bean eggs. These mini baskets made a charming centerpiece. Surround them, if you like, with the candleholders, or use the candleholders separately placed around a low bowl filled with spring flowers.

Brocaded eggs, covered with braid, pearls, and rhinestones.

Appliqué Technique in Brocade

After I got through playing with the fabric-covered "country cousin" eggs, I began wondering if this method would not work well with more elegant materials of textural interest.

Finding a lovely piece of gold brocade on sale, I bought it and started experimenting. This time I planned to use a goose egg and cover the whole egg.

I cut four pieces from the pattern given and glued them to the egg. The cloth, which was not stiff and fairly thin, went on easily, much to my surprise.

113

I covered each one of the four jointures with a strand of 3-mm. white pearls, banding the pearls on either side with heavy gold cord.

At the top of the egg I placed a tiny gold crown with a red stone in the center. (These are obtainable at craft or department stores.) This was banded with one row of gold cord and two rows of pearls to make a more pleasing composition.

One section of the egg was trimmed with a jewelry stone bearing the picture of the Mona Lisa. The jewelry stone was banded with 3-mm. pearls and eight rhinestones, placed around it and spaced about ¼-inch apart.

This egg was mounted on a metal egg stand which had been previously antiqued and sprayed with a protective finish before affixing the egg.

My next effort was a goose egg covered with blue silk brocade. This also went on smoothly but was of slightly heavier material and I found it necessary to make some tiny slashes as I worked. No problem about that, the banding trim would cover these.

The trim for this egg was aurora rhinestone (purchased by the yard at a department store). After running a strip of these down each section where the brocade joined, I banded the rhinestones with twisted silver cord. This completely covered any rough edges. If you cannot find aurora rhinestones, use white ones. They will give much the same effect though not quite so interesting.

The top of this egg was finished in exactly the same manner as before but with a small crown with a blue stone in the center.

The focal point of this egg was a blue and white cameo surrounded by a strand of white 3-mm. pearls. This was circled with twelve blue rhinestones, placed about ⅛-inch apart.

The stand for this egg was a gold plastic swan pillar that is normally used as a cake separator. It was 2½ inches high and came in sets of four. They are also obtainable in white and silver. For my purpose, I found the original gold color too bright. I used a water-base antiquing liquid in brown and toned it down, putting it on and wiping it off with a soft cloth until I obtained the effect I wanted.

When I was satisfied with the results, I sprayed it with a protective finish. Since these plastic swans are made of very lightweight material, I filled the inside with plaster of Paris to add weight and stability. The blown goose egg I used was not heavy but the trimmings were and these needed to be balanced by adding more weight to the stand.

When making these brocade-covered eggs, try to obtain goose eggs that are large and well-shaped so the trim will not appear crowded. The ones I used measured approximately 7 inches in diameter.

A very amusing egg of the appliqué type may be made by using a plain white egg (one that is as clean as possible). Cut black electrician's tape in irregular patterns and put them all over the egg—not too close so the white background will show. Mount this on a block of translucent lucite, or paint a block of plain wood black. Sometimes the simple, easy-to-make things are the most effective of all.

Football Eggs

My husband, like so many men, is a sports fan. I would never have thought of making up an egg to look like a football, but he did.

Probably because here in the Southwest so many things are made out of leather, I am charmed by this material, and find it easy to work with.

So, I hunted for and found two large chicken eggs. By adjusting the pattern, goose eggs or duck eggs would be just as easy to cover.

I cut a pattern similar to that used for the brocade eggs but used six pieces, instead of four, of reddish-brown garment leather as near "football color" as possible.

You will need to glue these on the egg carefully with no overlaps, fitting each piece closely as no covering can be used to hide mistakes. Leather, however, differs from other material and is easier to pull and finger-shape into place. Just work each section carefully and do not try to put on more than one at a time.

After all sections are put into place, take a piece of dark brown leather and cut eight tiny rectangles, gluing these in the center of the egg over one of the seams to simulate stitching.

I made two of these little footballs, for they were intended for use as a matching pair of bookends. (The diameter of the eggs is approximately $3^3/_4$ inches).

My husband is handy with woodworking tools so he cut four little 3-inch squares of $1/_2$-inch thick wood. Any wood will do, for these squares are completely covered. One end of each piece was beveled off and rounded.

Using the same shade of dark brown leather that I had used to simulate the stitching on the footballs, I cut leather strips to cover the sides of my blocks of wood, rounding them at the ends to fit. Two strips to each block is what you will need.

After the sides are covered glue the two pieces together, as shown in the illustration, using a strong contact glue. They may also be put together with very small nails but there is danger of splintering. Larger blocks of wood when the larger goose eggs are used could be nailed.

Beehive eggs in curtain ring stands.

After the jointure was firm, I covered each one of my pair with a continuous strip of white garment leather, running it around and gluing as I went.

I glued the footballs in a partially upright, leaning position to the leather.

My husband was quite pleased with the way this little suggestion worked out. The next idea he had was a sweet one. I listened. And here is what came of it.

Beehive Eggs

The first rule in my book of egg decoration is this: never lose sight of the true shape of the egg. Even when completely covered, as the beehive eggs are, they must still retain this shape and be distinguishable as such.

These eggs are prepared just like the others—pricked, blown, washed and drained. They are chicken eggs. It is not necessary to color them as they will be covered entirely with heavy cord.

Begin at the top of the egg and with the cord, make a close hairpin turn of about ¾ to one inch. Firmly secure with contact glue. Hold this for a few minutes if necessary to keep the cord from falling off before it has set. Then I like to let this first half turn firm up for about a half hour, depending on weather conditions—it will do this faster on a warm, dry day.

The reason for this is that considerable pull will be exerted on this first small section when you start to cover the egg.

Now, with the top secure, start spiraling the cord around the egg, gluing a few inches at a time as you go, and pressing the braid firmly to the egg and the preceding row so the effect will be smooth.

Finish at the bottom with another half turn. If you cannot cover the egg at the bottom don't worry about this; the beehive will set on a small pedestal base and this will not show.

After the braid has firmly set, glue or sew small chenille bees to the hive, one at the top to cover the end of the cord, and another peeking around the side. These charming little bees come in several assorted colors and may be obtained from craft stores or cake-decorating supply houses.

Now for the bases. Since these eggs are intended to be used for pincushions I chose a firm base that will not topple easily and found these at a small shop that repairs motors. They are small ball bearings about 1½ inch in diameter.

I painted my bases gold with Liquid Leaf, ran a strip of gold braid around the edges, and put a one-inch white plastic curtain ring on top for the beehive to rest in. I covered the ring, after the beehive was set, with a strip of flat gold braid wide enough to hide the ring and the jointure.

Of course, since these "pincushions" still have a real eggshell inside, any pins or needles put on them must be stuck in on a sidewise slant. They could also be made with an egg-shaped styrofoam base.

I made these beehive eggs in cerise, violet, and eggshell-colored cord. If you cannot find the color you want, buy white cord and dye it, letting it dry thoroughly for a day or two before you put it on the egg.

These beehives are patterned after the old-fashioned straw type which were once in common use and are so much more charming and decorative, though not as convenient as the box type used today.

CHAPTER THIRTEEN

Decorating with German Scrap

Have you ever lovingly leafed through an old scrapbook that belonged to your grandmother? Perhaps you found such a book in an attic you were exploring, or noticed one offered for sale in an antique shop. Maybe you looked at the price tag and found it was quite fantastic.

If so, you were probably fascinated by the quaint pictures in brilliant colors someone had spent hours pasting there for the entertainment of themselves and their families. You may have wondered where these pictures came from and if they were still available.

Where they came from was, most probably, Germany, for in the 1800s and on through the turn of the century, such colorful, embossed, die-cut pictures were chromolithographed there.

During those years people used the pictures to make their own greeting cards for Christmas, Easter, birthdays and other friendly or family occasion they wanted to make memorable. They were also used to decorate cakes and cookies and many were used on gift boxes. Often they were just collected in quantity to be pasted in scrapbooks; hence the name "Scrap Pictures."

To my delight I found that these same lithographed pictures are again being reproduced from the original plates in West Germany and are now imported to the United States by Brandon Memorabilia, Inc., 3 West 30th Street, New York, New York, 10001.

They have a number of motifs which include Easter, Christmas, and assorted flowers. They also offer gold motifs and gold medallions.

For the eggs I have decorated with scrap, I used the Easter, flowers, and gold-motif assortments. The flowers in this group come in several sizes and I used the smallest. I also cut apart some of the larger scrap which is designed to make this easy—the pictures come jointed together in flat sheets. To be used effectively, they must be cut apart and I find my curved-blade scissors useful for this.

Eggs to be decorated with scrap are prepared in the usual manner. I find it easiest to place the eggs in the food-coloring bath first and blow out the contents afterwards. I use a number of different shades of Cakolor, to obtain the deepest and richest color tones possible.

Leave the eggs in the coloring bath overnight if necessary. This coloring is harmless and when the contents are removed they may be saved and used. When this is done, set the eggs back upright in the carton to drain and dry.

Your first step is to choose your design. They are all so lovely that you may find this bewildering at first. However, there are several ways to plan.

It is always good to provide color contrast—blue flowers on a pink egg, violet on rose, even red on yellow can be surprisingly beautiful. I think where brilliant color is the keynote, the prettiest eggs have a definite theme all around the egg so that it will be attractive no matter how it lies in the basket or in whatever manner it is displayed.

Having decided on your design and color scheme, you may wish to add further interest by working in a butterfly, a bluebird, or even a small Easter bunny. For a Christmas theme there is an adorable, tiny, golden Santa complete with sleigh and reindeer. For Easter, there are golden crosses and butterflies.

One of the nicest things about this scrap is that it can be cut apart almost anywhere, even the larger pieces, and still look well. Keep a small box handy for odds and ends that you will not use immediately and save. That extra leaf, bud, or butterfly may be just what you will need later on somewhere else. Don't ever throw any of this lovely scrap away; even the tiniest pieces are useful to place over the blow holes at the ends of the eggs.

Cutting: As a child I loved to cut out paper dolls and this part of the decoration is still so enjoyable that I like to linger over it. I could spend hours just cutting the materials and moving them around to form designs. It intrigues me so much that I never tire of it.

However, those who are not accustomed to this type of work may find it tedious in the beginning, so I would suggest that you do not try to

Eggs decorated with German Scrap, displayed in antique bride's basket.

stay at it too long. It should be a pleasure to you, so if you get tired, stop for a while and do something else. Return to it when you are rested and anxious to begin again.

For the actual cutting there are a number of tools which have been developed specially for cutting paper, such as decoupage scissors which have extremely sharp and slender points. They come with either a straight or a slightly curved blade. Try both for you may find one easier to use than the other.

Personally, I like the curved blade best, but you should try different pairs until you find the one that is just right for you. If you have a special problem such as arthritis or very large hands, this should be taken into account. Sometimes men enjoy this work, too—if they have a pair of scissors of a size which suits them.

There is something else to consider. Are you right- or left-handed? Scissors are made for left-handed folks, too. If you need these, search until you find a pair; they are available.

Now, begin cutting by holding the scissors in your cutting hand with the thumb and third finger—let your index finger rest under the cutting blade—enabling you to guide your work. Relax and enjoy this experience—if you make a mistake, there's always glue or a tiny scrap of scotch tape.

Use your cutting hand to open and close your scissors. Keep this hand in one position and feed the paper quite slowly into the scissors. Curve the paper back and forth following all the contours of the print.

Much of your scrap will already be cut out, but it is important to know how to cut properly as you may need to make some of the prints smaller in order to have them look well on the eggs and in proper proportion. Also, some of the prints have a fine line of white around them where the printing colors did not quite cover the paper. It is important to remove this so your eggs will have a professional look. It is also good to know the proper cutting technique so that intricate bits such as the wings of birds and edges of the butterfly wings are cut correctly.

You can cut a serrated edge by wiggling the paper back and forth, feeding it slowly and carefully into your scissors as you do so. This will give you the finely scalloped edge so often seen on a butterfly wing, and contribute further to the professional, yet natural, look you are working toward.

Work underneath your paper as much as possible. Point the curved blades away from your cutting, for this will make it easier for you to see your work as you go along.

For placing your scrap on the eggs there is one more thing you must do before putting on the glue. Some of this beautifully embossed paper is rather heavy, especially the gold motifs.

In order to overcome this slight disadvantage, I turn my design over and on the reverse side, which I find easier to see, i make very tiny slashes $1/8$ inch or less, all around my paper. By doing this you will find they fit nicely to the curve of the egg.

Now, using white glue and my fingers, I cover the underside of the scrap, smoothing it on evenly so that every tiny bit is covered with a thin, even coat. Keep a bowl of water handy and a small towel and wash your fingers frequently so you won't get all "stuck up."

After you have smoothed the glue on the first piece of the design, place it on the egg. If the egg is to have a focal spot like a cross, butterfly, or Santa and sleigh, put this piece on first. It may be laid on either horizontally or vertically depending on the size of the picture or on how you plan to use it. These eggs can be hung from a tree or displayed in a bowl or basket.

You may pick your scrap up with your fingers or, if it is a very tiny piece, you may find tweezers will be of help.

Tap the paper down lightly. Now just moisten a small piece of lintless cloth or a small cosmetic sponge. Pat the picture carefully, pressing out any excess glue and wiping it off. Pat gently until the pic-

German Scrap, a fascinatingly beautiful material to work with, for all major holidays.

ture is perfectly clean, otherwise glue will dull the picture if any remains on the surface.

This is where this scrap with its glossy, hard surface really shows its superiority over other pictures which may have been cut from magazines or Christmas cards. It will not tear easily as other paper does and is far easier to work with.

You will find as you work that the tiny slashes you have made will permit you to fit the picture firmly and perfectly to the countour of the egg—top, bottom, and sides—no matter how the individual egg happens to be shaped.

I have used chicken eggs for this project because the shells seem to take the dye better than goose or duck eggs. Of course you could use the larger eggs if you wanted to, but if you do, I would suggest that they be painted in suitable colors rather than dyed.

Depending on which method you have used for blowing the eggs, you will have one or two holes to cover. Be sure these are completely covered with tiny bits of scrap so they will not show. If you find some of the holes a little large, you can fill them with plaster of Paris if you like before putting on the scrap.

After you have put on your first piece of scrap let it dry thoroughly before putting on another especially if you are working with a small egg, for you may dislodge it by handling before it is completely dry.

Whenever I am doing this type of egg decoration, I like to work with several eggs at a time, allowing the first one to dry and taking up another. Working on five or six at a time lets you make faster progress and thus many eggs can be decorated in a few hours' time.

To keep your materials separated, I would suggest that you cut the pieces intended for each egg. Have a couple of clean TV dinner trays handy, the three-section kind, and put each design or color in a separate section. By doing this you will avoid confusion—you can work rapidly and make good use of the time you have allotted to the gluing operation.

As you will note from the illustration, I do not attempt to cover the entire egg with the pictures, for the background color (you may even leave the eggs white, if you like) adds much to the charm of the composition.

Decoupaging—there are a number of finishes to choose from and you may like one better than the other. I just happen to like the eggshell finish best. This has a very slight gloss, almost flat, and will give your work a hand-rubbed look.

Eggshell has just a slight tinge of color, just enough to mellow your work and give the eggs the slightly antique look desirable for this old-fashioned material. It will also tone down some of the very bright hues of the scrap and give just a suggestion of an ivory tinge to your white eggs.

On the other hand, you may prefer a clear vinyl finish which will keep the true colors. Clear vinyl is colorless, has an extremely high gloss, and will produce a very hard surface. Set your eggs on an egg rack for spraying. The tiny hole can be plugged up later and touched with spray.

You may even wish to combine two finishes, painting the eggs first to give them an ivory look and then spraying them for the brilliant glossy finish.

The rich colors of these eggs and their decorations make them particularly suitable for ballantine. This material consists of small, hard, translucent glass balls which reflect light. I like to paint the entire egg slightly with white glue or a transparent adhesive and sprinkle the ballantine over it with a salt shaker. Any that falls off can be saved and reused if no particles of glue cling to it.

If you like, you may run a knitting needle through one end of the egg for a convenient handle to enable you to turn the egg easily as you work. Working over a small box will keep the ballantine from scattering too much and keep it from being wasted. It is not an expensive material, but I am a thrifty soul and never like to discard anything that may be used again.

Another type of finish which also tones down the brilliant colors is pearl lacquer. This imparts a pearlized finish to the undecorated areas of the eggshell as well as the pictures, and the effect is very interesting. I do not like to use this over the gold motifs, but for the flower pictures it is beautiful.

Use any finish that suits your fancy, but do use a protective finish of some type, for these eggs are lovely enough to become, in time, heirlooms and may be cherished for many generations to come. Don't forget to put your name or initials on them somewhere, as an identification adds greatly to their value.

CHAPTER FOURTEEN

The Eggshells and I

This is a fun project to be approached with a light heart and lots of eggshells—preferably in many colors. Every morning I saved two eggshells from the breakfast eggs, rinsed them under the faucet to get out every bit of the white still clinging to the inside, and carefully broke the thin "skin" at the end of the eggshell. Unless this is done, the color will not take on that part of the shell. I also saved the shells from the chicken eggs I broke in other decorating projects. I do not find goose eggs practical for mosaic pictures as the shells are hard to color and more difficult to crush.

For a couple of weeks I simply kept my shells in pint-sized fruit jars each about half full of liquid dye. You can use Easter Egg dye, food colors, Rit, or any type of dye that suits your fancy for obtaining a particular shade. My preference is the Cakolor paste colors which come in 21 superb shades including black.

These paste colors are very strong, since they are intended primarily for cake frosting, but will mix readily with water for coloring the eggshells. After placing the coloring in the water, stir until dissolved.

The intensity of color depends on how much you use and also the length of time they are left in the coloring bath. If I want very deep shades I leave them in overnight.

When the shells are the right color, I take them out of the dye and place them on newspapers to allow them to dry thoroughly for at least 24 hours. They may be dried more quickly by placing them in a warm oven (a very slow oven and check frequently so they will not be discolored) or near a fire.

When completely dry, I crumble them in my hands onto the newspaper which I now place on a hard surface. Putting a cardboard or more newspaper on top of them so they will not shatter in all directions, I go over them with a rolling pin until the desired fineness is reached. After each "rolling" I push the shells into a little heap with my fingers as this gets the larger pieces on the top of the heap so they will be crushed also.

Putting the shells in a blender will reduce them to powder and, for very fine work, this is also useful.

One of the things I noticed was that in the coloring process the inside of the shell always tinted much darker than the outside. This does not matter. In the rolling process the colors are evened out and mixing several days' accumulation of shells of the same color tone will not be objectionable—they will all blend pleasingly.

Also, the dried shells which you have broken and accumulated from other egg projects will color just as readily as fresh shells will; just be sure they have no glue or paint on them for this will prevent effective coloring.

Though I found from time to time that I needed additional colors or additional shells of the same color when I started to work on a picture or another object to be decorated, I accumulated most of my colors by a steady, daily process of just making a few at a time. I stored my crushed shells in small clear jars or jelly glasses with tops. I tried to have a full palette of colors before I started my first picture.

Since this whole project was one of complete whimsy, I decided to use backgrounds made entirely of wallpaper. If you haven't looked at the new papers lately you are missing something, they are just gorgeous.

One of the wallpaper establishments I contacted was kind enough to give me two of their huge books of sample patterns. Each book contained dozens of patterns appropriate to every room in the house with choices of style, color, and texture almost unlimited. If you cannot obtain one of these books from your local dealer, then ask to look through them and buy a roll of the wallpaper of your choice.

The sheets I worked with were approximately 18 × 22 inches in size and I mounted those I selected on a backing of stiff corrugated cardboard. Cardboard boxing will do fine for this—you can probably find these at the grocery store.

Tiny owls set against rippled wallpaper background that adds realism to the night sky.

For the picture of the "Loving Owls" I chose a background paper with a delightful ripple effect of light blue, deep blue, and gold which gives the effect of a night sky. I further enhanced this by a golden eggshell moon.

The first step in making my inlay picture is, of course, the drawing. Since it is not wise to make erasures on the wall paper, I do not draw directly on it. I make my drawing on thin cardboard (the kind that comes from the laundry in shirts is good to use) and, after achieving the correct proportions, I cut it out and place it exactly where I want on the wallpaper background. In this way I can move the various pieces around until I have a pleasing, well-proportioned composition.

In cutting, use the same technique suggested in the chapter on decorating with German Scrap, making your pattern as clear and well-shaped as possible. You can even cut the pattern apart piece by piece after you have drawn the outline if it will help you and save the work of redrawing.

After I am satisfied with my design, I draw around my pattern, using a soft lead pencil which I also use for the detailing. Next, I use a felt tip *waterproof* (this is important) pen to go over the pencil lines so they can be easily seen.

I prefer to work with only one color of crushed eggshell at a time, deciding which areas I will color brown, white, orange, blue or whatever. Since the owls needed lots of brown I started with this first.

Using Elmer's School Glue with the conical tip, I filled in the "brown" areas with white glue, not too heavily or it will run out under the eggshells. Using my fingers, I sprinkled the crushed eggshells into these places and patted them down gently after a few minutes so that more shells would adhere.

I let this first application completely dry, allowing it to rest both during the working period and the drying time on a flat surface so the glue would not run. Depending on how heavily you have applied the glue and the humidity or dryness of the weather, it should take an hour or two to dry.

When dry, I stood the picture up vertically, tapping it gently so the excess shell would fall off. As long as you do not get your colors mixed you need not discard the shells. Return them to the jar to be used again. (Even when my colors mix I save the varicolored bits in a separate jar to be used as background material. This works especially well for boxes and purses to be discussed later.)

Proceed with each color in turn, using the same method until all areas you wish to fill are covered. When thoroughly dry I outlined the picture of the owls with a fine camel hair brush dipped in black India ink. This will give emphasis and contrast to the picture as the various colors are outlined and detail added.

The intense black of the vines over the moon and the tree limb the two owls are perched on is a "crafty" touch of black embroidery thread, glued down in long strands. Cut short bits for the smaller limbs, gradually filling in the outlined space.

It is not absolutely necessary, but I often find that I can produce a richer effect by going over my areas to be "eggshelled" twice. After the first coat of shells dries, I again apply white glue and a second coat of shells.

If this second coat is applied only to certain selected areas the result will be an interesting raised effect which gives the unusual texture of the shells added importance, similar to the sculptured relief look of cut velvet.

In the "Loving Owls" picture I went over the moon, the leaves, and the eyes of the owls twice.

My Pink Elephant, juggling the ABCs, was worked out in exactly the same manner as the Loving Owls. I drew my pattern, cut it out of cardboard, and then outlined it on the wallpaper background. The large, block letter ABCs were handled in the same way. I moved them around until I felt the composition was pleasing and the letters far enough apart so they would not look crowded. This picture measures 18½ × 16½ inches. The small, patterned flower background, predominantly blue, is in harmony with the subject.

The simple outlines of the "Dancing Donkey" were drawn on a muted green background and the flowers and butterfly added to give a look of sprightliness and springtime.

Again my largest area of color was brown and this was filled in first with the other colors added later. The saddle, bridle, eye, flower wreath, and butterfly were eggshelled twice. The black outlines and the donkey's mane were emphasized with black India ink. The picture measures 13 × 17 inches.

My last picture, the "Fruit Bowl," was a little more elaborate than the others. After filling in all the fruit and the bowl with eggshells in the planned colors, I went over each piece with a second application of white glue and eggshells. I paid special attention to the grapes where I achieved a sculptured effect by raising several of these up slightly higher than the others with a third application.

The dimensional effect of the picture was further emphasized by my choice of the wallpaper background which, with its textured pattern of avocado green, provided a perfect setting for the delicious-looking fruit.

After the brown shells of the bowl were completely dry, I added a touch of Liquid Gold, dividing the bowl into panels outlined in black India ink. The centers of the panels were painted gold with the brown shells providing contrast. Finally the bowl was outlined with black embroidery thread glued down carefully (so none got on the paper except at the very edge of the bowl) with white glue.

To make my fruit look more realistic I used shells which I had colored in the deepest possible shades which were further enhanced by touches of watercolor tinting. To achieve this I mixed my watercolors with a very small amount of white acrylic paint. You may use acrylic paints entirely if you prefer, but I like the many different shades possible which the Grumbacher watercolors can give me. These produce a soft, luscious effect—making you want to reach out and touch the fruit.

The pineapples were done in three tones of shells—green, brown, and yellow. I used red for the apples, orange for the oranges (with shadowy touches of brown), yellow for the pears, etc.

The grapes, which appear to have the characteristic "bloom" of this fruit, were done in purple and blue and for several of these I mixed purple and blue shells which aided in softening the effect.

To frame this picture I selected a very plain wooden frame and

Fruit Picture (right). Fruit may be given more realism by shading lightly with acrylic paint or colored inks (below).

Crushed, dyed eggshell make bright and decorative pictures.

finished it out in gold leaf. Directions for doing this have been given in a previous chapter.

For a picture, such as the "Pink Elephant" with ABCs I would suggest a very simple, not too wide, frame of black or white. This picture would be most entertaining in a small child's room. The "Loving Owls" and the "Dancing Donkey" could be used almost any place.

Don't for one minute think that these pictures are hard to do. An easy way to learn to use your materials is to choose a wallpaper which has a patterned background of flowers or some other design you like—something that does not have too much small detail—for your first picture.

Follow the outlines with the conical tip of your glue bottle and then fill in the centers with just enough glue to cover. Then fill in the colors —sprinkling them on with your fingers. Pat down gently so the shells will adhere.

Another easy way to get your designs, if you find drawing a bit difficult, is to get a child's coloring book that has simple pictures with heavy black outlines. Choose something you find amusing, cut it out, and, using white glue, paste it on your wallpaper background. Following the lines already there, fill in with glue and sprinkle on your eggshells. It's fun.

In fact, these pictures are so much fun and so easy to do that—once I got started—I just couldn't seem to stop making them. I'm positively greedy about eggshells—I save every one of them 365 days out of the year, and I even have other members of the family and friends helping me.

Being a confirmed egger and proud of it, I like to advertise this fact. Is there a better way to do this than to carry a purse decorated with eggshells? The one I made always excites comment and curiosity wherever I go. Everyone wants to know "What is it made of?" and "How do you do it?"

Here's how: look for a fairly large wooden purse, one with flat sides and top; curves are not practical with this method. Each panel must be considered separately yet be a part of the whole, a pleasing composition with one theme just as you would for a decoupage design.

I am particularly fond of bright butterflies and decided to use these along with flowers on each panel and the top. Most craft shops carry these with real wings and paper bodies and they are entirely suitable for pictures, boxes or purses, if handled with care.

I began by outlining the first panel with white glue and then filling in the entire panel with a thin coat. The butterflies should be handled as little as possible, so you will decide where they are going to go before you place them—once on the glue they should stay there. Press them down gently so they will make good contact and be careful not to tear the delicate wings.

The flowers I used were some that I had previously dried in the silica sand. For use on the purse I pressed them flat in a large catalog. These were now placed on the panel.

Actually, this purse is the easiest project of all to make, for all you need do now is sprinkle on the eggshells. The background can be any color you want it to be. While mine is predominantly blue, it is actually a mixture of many colors; there are tiny bits of purple, red, yellow, and rose which add interest as the eye picks them up.

I cannot emphasize too strongly that you must let each panel dry thoroughly before going on to the next one; 24 hours is not too long. When the first panel is completely dry, spray it with the clear, glossy finish. Each coat thereafter will make your butterflies more durable.

If you find the spray darkens your flowers and butterflies too much, there's nothing in the rules to keep you from touching them up here and there with acrylic paint—*after the first spraying.* Use a small camel-hair brush and brighten them up before you spray again.

Since purses get a lot of wear I gave mine 30 coats of spray, light

Cracked shell purse. Paint in any color you like.

coats at ten-minute intervals on a warm, dry day and it has stood up well.

Depending on how your purse is made, the enamel trim should be applied last after all spraying is complete. For mine I used a dark blue celluloid, very hard finish enamel of the type used for painting fishing lures. This is very durable and will stand up well under wear. I gave the trim, handle and knob two coats of this and, since it is waterproof, handling does not bother it at all. I really did find some wonderful things in that box of paint my husband uses for painting his fishing equipment.

There is virtually no end to all the exciting possibilities of covering useful objects with eggshells. Try putting butterflies and flowers on a wooden wall plaque. Or finish out cigar boxes with this technique and use them on your dresser (or your daughter's) to hold hair curlers and other odds and ends. They're great "neatner-uppers."

Though it seems like gilding the lily you can even coat eggs themselves with the shells by first painting them in sections with white glue and then rolling them in the shells. Spray after drying and you will have some mighty unusually decorated eggs. These are particularly attractive when several different colors are displayed.

CHAPTER FIFTEEN

From Fun to Fabulous

These eggs run all the way up and down the scale and back again. Just when I think I've done everything to eggs except dip them in hot chocolate, another idea occurs to me and I'm off and running. I have a sneaking suspicion that just when I close the covers of this book I'll have the most fantastic one of all and then I'll sit here mentally kicking myself for not thinking of it sooner. (By now I'm getting positively egg-centric!)

Be that as it may, here are some designs that I would like to share before I come to the last chapter. Believe it or not—that last chapter also concerns decorating *you* while you are decorating the eggs!

Fruit and Flower Plaque

People sometimes jokingly call eggs "hen fruit"—perhaps that was how this particular idea for a picture originated in my mind.

This picture can be any size you care to make it, but I would suggest that a fairly large background and frame would look the best. My frame, painted a dark brown with two coats of walnut enamel, measures 18 × 24 inches. Of course you can use a square frame if you prefer but I liked this one because the oval suggests the shape of the egg and the curve of the frame is in harmony with the picture it encloses.

The actual picture without the frame measures 13 × 19 inches. I cut a piece of corrugated cardboard boxing this size and covered it with gold brocade, pulling it as tightly as possible and securing it to the backing with masking tape.

For the central design, do the following: using the Dremel, cut five chicken eggs in half, horizontally. Drain, wash, and dry. Place each half on thin cardboard and draw around shell, numbering shell and cardboard as you work. Cut cardboard and glue to shell. Trim any protruding edges when dry.

Paint each egg with purple celluloid enamel, using a ¼-inch flat brush. Always brush in one direction. Three thin coats should give you complete coverage; if not, go over the eggs again. This enamel has the endearing feature of drying very quickly. I allow about half an hour between coats.

When egg is well covered and dry, paint with transparent adhesive. Using a salt shaker, shake on ballantine. This gives the effect of the attractive "bloom" often seen on big purple plums when they are at their delicious best.

Now take two more eggs, bantam or guinea hen if you can get them. If not, use chicken eggs. Cut them in two as before. If you are using chicken eggs, cut away a portion of the shell so you will have smaller "fruit." Paint shells as before but use dark blue celluloid enamel. When complete, coat with ballantine.

Remember back in the chapter on "Eggs on the Half Shell" we had one-quarter of a goose egg left when we made the Lavabo? Back this first on one side and then the other with a piece of thin cardboard cut to fit. Paint with yellow enamel and sprinkle with ballantine. This makes our "banana."

The "lemon" is one half of a chicken egg cut vertically, backed with cardboard, painted yellow and ballantined.

"Apples" are doors cut from alcove eggs and saved. One is a goose egg and one a chicken egg. These were backed with cardboard, painted deep red and sprinkled as were the others.

Leaves are cut from shells of chicken, goose and duck eggs. Chicken eggs are easiest to cut just after discarding contents while shells are still moist. Don't worry if some of the edges are a bit ragged. Leaves are all edged with green velveteen cut on the bias both to strengthen and trim. Leaves are also painted with green enamel and ballantine is used.

If your picture is either larger or smaller than mine you will need more or less fruit. Also, if your frame is square, round or oblong this will make a difference in the positioning of your material.

Work out your design before you glue your fruit down. Be sure they are completely dry so you can move them around like chessmen on a board, trying them in different positions until you get the "fruit" just the way you want.

After this is to your liking, take up each piece in turn, spread contact adhesive on the cardboard and return to the correct place, gently pressing the piece down. It is not likely that the ballantine will rub off if it is well dried; however, if it does, you can apply another thin coat of adhesive to the spot and shake on more after the fruit is in position.

After all the fruit is in place, you can make your picture much prettier and more graceful by adding a few vine-like tendrils of brown embroidery thread. After positioning, glue down with jewelry cement which dries clear.

You will note bare spaces between the fruit. I filled these in by using tiny straw "star" flowers (purchasable at most craft shops). Cut flower stems in staggered lengths, put glue on the lower portion of the stems and insert them under the eggs and leaves and let them extend as shown. Mass them in little groups between the eggs in the central part of the picture. To do this, put on a drop or two of white glue, break the flower heads off and press them into the glue. Put a few tiny flowers here and there on the leaves.

These tiny flowers give an airy effect to the picture. The colors I used were red, burnt orange, and green with an occasional white or yellow. The flowers need not lie perfectly flat. In fact, I think they look better if they are slightly raised from the background and will fall into the position naturally when they are inserted behind the leaves and fruit.

"Magic" Mushrooms

Have you ever tried to decorate eggs with three, huge Siamese cats watching every move you make? That's how I work most of the time—every move I make is catalogued in their deep blue eyes and, if the spirit moves them, they occasionally jump on my table to be of assistance, even though they know I take a dim view of this offer.

Inevitably, wreckage occurs. Such were the circumstances one day when I had a number of blown eggshells on the table. Called to the

Magic Mushrooms, colorful and decorative.

phone, I returned to see all three cats batting the shells around and having a wonderful time.

Siamese are smart, they knew they shouldn't be up there. Simultaneously all three leaped to the floor and eggshells scattered in all directions. I should have been angry but I wasn't—I had to laugh at their expressions of complete innocence as they surveyed the damage and me from a safe distance.

I sat there spinning one of the broken shells around on my finger, and suddenly the idea hit me that it looked just like one of the little toadstools that spring up in the grass overnight when we have warm, humid days in the spring.

After strengthening the shells I cut them so the edges would be smooth, and painted them with three coats of red celluloid enamel. For the stems I obtained some dowels 3/8 inch in diameter and cut these in lengths varying from 3 to 4 inches. I filled the cup of the egg with plaster of Paris, inserted the dowels (previously painted white) while the plaster was still moist, and let dry.

As I happened to have on hand a few half shells from bantam eggs I treated these in the same manner as the chicken eggs, using smaller dowels and a few curved twigs.

When the Plaster had set, I edged each mushroom with silver fringe as heading, letting the fringe extend downward. I then dotted white iridescent sequins on the mushrooms, placing a bead in each for greater interest and to cover up the tiny hole.

To display my mushrooms I bought a round piece of Styrofoam 12 inches in diameter and sprayed it with gray Testors Spray Play Enamel which will not dissolve the styrofoam.

When my platform was dry, I simply pressed the dowels down into the Styrofoam, letting some of them lean a little for a more natural look. I added a few white, rounded quartz pebbles picked up at the beach and a pair of amusing white mice. Elves, leprechauns or other tiny animals could be used just as effectively.

Time of Day in a Goose Egg

For this I used a large goose egg with a well-rounded shape. The "clock" is a man's wrist watch with gold numerals, as I planned to gold-leaf both the egg and the stand.

I laid the watch, face down, on cardboard and drew a pattern from it. When you draw around something, the pattern will be just slightly larger and you must allow for this or your circle will be too large when you again use it to cut the opening for the watch in the egg. It is better to make the opening for the watch a little smaller than necessary and gradually enlarge it, using the smallest steel cutter that comes with the Dremel Moto-Tool kit for this job.

Keep fitting the watch as you work and when the hole is exactly the right size, put the watch aside and cut a door in the back of the egg. This door, which is to be hinged, should be large enough so that the watch can be introduced through it and placed in position inside the egg. (See chapter on Cutting the Shells for directions.)

Depending on how your watch is made, there are several ways of placing the watch so it will stay in position. It may be put on a metal stand or slipped through a piece of flexible cardboard which will curve to the shape of the egg and hold the watch in position. Whatever method you choose, the watch should be removable for winding.

The decoration for this watch egg is Rococo, as bejeweled as I could make it. First, I gold-leafed the egg by the process already described. I then outlined the watch with two rows of the narrowest gold braid I could find. Be careful here; you do not want to overwhelm the watch

Goose egg watch holder, decorated with braid and pearls.

with something too large. This was followed by a row of strung pearls.

Two bands of aurora rhinestones cross at the top and bottom. One strand was placed first and glued. The second strand was cut into three pieces to avoid the heavy, cumbersome look which would have resulted had the rhinestones actually been crossed. Butt the pieces up carefully and exactly against the first strand for a continuous look and it will not be apparent that the strand has been cut. The rhinestones were edged on either side with gold cord, slightly larger than that used around the rim of the watch.

A row of pearls was next placed around the sides of the egg, vertically, with gold cord edging on either side.

The finial is a rhinestone button with a pearl rim around it.

The stand for this watch was once actually a small clock. I bought it for ten cents at a tag sale several years ago and put it in my box for things-to-be-used later. I gold-leafed this stand, following the same directions I have given for the picture frame in a previous chapter. It was then decorated with white pearls and gold cord.

Now, here is another place where it is very useful to know how to build up your own egg stands, so they can be proportioned exactly and given the correct height.

Using the ornamental top of a cosmetic jar to start with, I built the stand up, piece by piece, with the metal cap from an aerosol can and three small plastic curtain rings.

I kept trying to place the egg as I went along so I would get the proportions of both height and spacing exactly right. When both were achieved to my satisfaction I started the decoration of the stand itself, using white pearls and gold cord completely to cover my framework. It is a good idea to paint the framework with Liquid Leaf before covering so that no hint of color will peep through and spoil the effect.

Of course the door in the back of the egg should be banded also with simple gold cord and a door pull of some sort glued to it. Mine is a pearl that was part of an earring.

When stand and egg are finished, the egg should be glued in place with a good contact adhesive. Hold it for a few minutes until it stays in place.

Eggs Oriental

Driftwood is one of the natural materials that has great appeal to me and when I picked up this piece its writhing and tortured contours immediately suggested a Chinese dragon.

For this composition I chose two goose eggs, as nearly alike in size and shape as possible, each one approximately 7 inches in diameter. The match holder is half of a guinea egg. Guinea eggs have shells almost as thick and durable as goose eggs.

The incense holder, top cut and hinged, was decorated in a manner extremely, almost deceptively, simple. I gave it five very thin, coats of red celluloid enamel, being extra careful to avoid any buildup for there would be no trimmings to cover up my errors. When this was dry, I

Twisted driftwood and smooth eggs, a contrast in forms.

edged the egg, both the top and bottom piece, with twisted gold cord. This was all the ornamentation it would receive.

For the interior I mixed a small quantity of plaster of Paris to put in the bottom to weight the egg. This was covered by a cardboard platform glued to the plaster. The interior of the egg was then painted with Liquid Leaf Gold. When dry, a band of twisted gold braid was run around the edge of the cardboard to hide slight irregularities.

The incense burner was a little more complicated but not at all difficult to achieve if directions are carefully followed. One of the things I like best about my Dremel Moto-Tool is the ease with which it can be used for small, delicate work, and after the drawings for the four apertures in the egg were accomplished cutting was no problem.

First, draw four lines, dividing the egg into four equal parts from top to bottom of the egg. Draw a triangle in each one of the sections, curving the lines slightly to the shape of the egg. My triangles measure approximately one inch across the bottom and are about 1¼ inches high. When these are drawn, erase all lines except the triangles.

Using the lower part of the triangle as a guide, draw a horizontal line around the egg at the approximate center where it will be cut.

I used a blown egg for this so there were no contents to be disposed of. The four triangles were cut first and the cut around the center of the egg was made last.

This egg was painted with five coats of red enamel just like the incense holder. I also made a cardboard platform for the egg in the same way, with the plaster of Paris in the bottom for weight.

The interior of the egg was then entirely covered, both pieces, with liquid solder, with special attention given to coating the cardboard platform. I built up a small, rounded depression in the center to hold the stick or cone of incense.

Each of the four apertures was decorated with a small piece of metal filigree, cut from a necklace and firmed into place with the liquid solder.

Each of the windows and the top and bottom pieces of the egg were edged with twisted gold cord.

The finial on the incense burner is a tiny, ivory-colored monkey which I cut from a key chain found at a department store. It is edged with one row of twisted gold cord.

To complete this composition, I added a small matchholder. This is made of half a guinea egg, also painted red and with the interior strengthened by adding liquid solder.

After deciding where I wanted to position each piece on my driftwood, I glued small plastic curtain rings to the wood to hold each egg. I then gave the driftwood and the curtain rings three coats of black celluloid enamel, letting the enamel dry well between each coat.

This attractive and unusual decoration is not only charming but useful. Placed anywhere in the room it is a great conversation piece, and as the smoke from the incense curls out through the four apertures, it dominates the entire room.

This set of three Oriental pieces would be equally lovely done in turquoise blue and gold or any other color that would harmonize well with the decor of your room. Metal findings similar to the ones I used for the windows of the incense burner are obtainable from craft shops.

If you cannot find a piece of driftwood to your liking, try placing the set on one of the popular poplar plaques—this could be either painted black or left in its natural wood tones.

An Egg for Your Valentine

This idea has many possibilities, for Valentines are always a popular gift. Their history is more ancient than most of us realize though their

A lovely egg for a Valentine.

selection is no longer the serious matter that it once was—especially in the Victorian era.

When I was a child in school we used to look forward to Valentine's Day each year for we each drew out of a box the name of a schoolmate to whom we were then honor-bound to give a Valentine. This was a nice way of doing things and made sure nobody was left out.

Little did we know how ancient was the origin of this custom. Drawing a Valentine by lot is believed to be a survival of one of the rites from Roman times, very possibly a part of the ceremony connected with the Lupercalia.

It is believed that during this festival the names of young women were put in a box to be drawn out by the young men guided purely by luck. This custom seems to have skipped a few centuries and been revived during Victorian times when names were again drawn by lot.

The name drawn had much significance and would remain a Valentine for an entire year. This situation often led to a betrothal, adding to the aura of romance surrounding this delightful custom.

We youngsters didn't take it that seriously, but we did have a lot of fun with our little Valentine box and cherished the Valentines we received.

Valentine motifs seem to have partaken of just about everything, but very early, flowers, hearts and doves seem to have emerged as the most popular. Fat little cupids, a young couple walking or talking together, all surrounded by much lace, are also seen in very early models.

One particularly pretty Valentine of 1797 which I studied has a number of little lace paper ovals, for all the world like the shape of an egg, and this and the other motifs influenced my decision to see what I could come up with. The pictured egg is the result and here is how I made it:

You will need one large duck egg, cut to form a heart-shaped opening. The point of the heart should be at the larger end of the egg. To get this the right shape, draw it in with a lead pencil and cut with the Dremel.

Cover the egg with red velveteen following the directions previously given for alcove eggs.

Cut a bias strip of red velveteen 1/2-inch wide and place it around the egg opening, 1/4-inch outside and 1/4-inch inside.

Position a row of 2 mm. white pearls around the edge of the egg.

Place a row of narrow gold cord next to the pearls.

Leave a narrow strip, about 1/4-inch, of red velvet showing and place another row of gold cord.

Behind this (fourth row from opening), place another row of 2-mm. pearls.

The fifth row is again gold cord.

Now, gather white nylon lace, 1/2-inch wide, and even this on your gathering thread, secure with pins to hold in place just behind the last row of gold cord.

Sew lace to gold cord, evening with your fingers as you go.

Interior of Valentine Egg

Make a paste of white glue and a little water. Using a stiff brush, coat the inside of the egg, bringing the mixture up to the rim of red velveteen inside egg.

Shake white crystals (Diamond Dust) over glue while still moist. Let

The Bullock Cart, an attractive centerpiece for a festive table.

set a few minutes. Shake out excess (this can be reused, so save it) and let dry.

I made the ornament for the inside of the egg by cutting a small heart out of cardboard (about one inch in diameter), and covering it with a piece of red velveteen. On the front I placed a row of 2-mm. white pearls around the edge.

On the back of the cardboard I attached a small piece of flexible wire about 2 inches long. I rolled the excess wire into a tiny base which was covered by wrapping it with flat gold braid sewed into place. This was edged with pearls.

After gluing a white dove to the red heart, I positioned the base inside the egg, allowing the little heart to stand out about ½-inch from the back of the egg, giving a three-dimensional effect.

The Base

Start with one of the small glass coasters used under the feet of furniture to prevent them from marking the surface of rugs.

Take three plastic lace hearts and glue them to the rim of the coaster; point upward in a slanting position. When the hearts are firmly in place,

Toothpick holders can be made using various small animals.

glue a 1½-inch gold plastic curtain ring over the points and set the Valentine egg in this ring.

Note how the curved heart cut from the egg exactly follows the shape of the white lace heart base, thus achieving a unified-looking whole.

This same design could be used for dozens of different Valentines simply by changing the interior decoration of the egg. And, though red and white are traditionally the "Valentine colors," there is no law that says you cannot use other colors as well. I have made these eggs in blue, green, yellow, and even orange.

The Bullock Cart

This design is touched with the magic of Mexico. The little metal cart and the amusing black and gold "Ferdinand" measure approximately 12 inches long. The "strawberries" are guinea eggs.

To prepare the eggs you can, using the dental burr of the Dremel, cut a hole in the top and bottom and blow out the contents. Or, you can cut them in half, as I did, wash the interior, and, when dry, glue the eggs back together again. Since guinea eggs have thick shells, this is easy to do, so I prefer this method, and there is no hole in the bottom of the egg to be filled.

After the eggs have received five coats of red celluloid enamel, the cutting line is barely noticeable and the eggs have a hard, brilliant waterproof finish. A strawberry is the only fruit that I know of that has its seeds on the *outside.* To simulate these seeds, I glued yellow seed beads in a random pattern all over the eggs.

To make the leaves and the stems, I used green felt in the shade usually called "Kelly" green. The stems are simply thin strips of felt crossed over and glued down to the edge. I cut two leaves of green felt and sewed them to the stems, pinching them together as I sewed so they would stand up a bit.

I also cut a rounded oval of green felt to be placed in the bottom of the cart. When the strawberries were placed on this, they looked even more brilliant by contrast.

You might prefer to make some of these strawberries for use in a fruit bowl. Paint some rounded chicken eggs purple as you did for the flower and fruit picture and, perhaps a few oblong eggs can be used as "lemons." This would make a very unusual centerpiece and could be used at any season of the year.

Eggs for Toothpick Holders

Among the many small receptacles that eggs can be used for, toothpick holders should not be overlooked. By various means the eggs can be strengthened and also made washable.

The first holder, presided over by Flower, the little skunk, is two-thirds of a guinea egg. The inside of the egg was covered with liquid solder and painted with three coats of dark green waterproof enamel. The outside of the egg was covered with rows of narrow, ¼-inch straw braid in two colors. It was glued on one row at a time and not spiraled—ending at the same spot each time. The ball bearing in which the holder was placed was simply painted with black celluloid enamel and given no other ornamentation.

The little figurine and the holder were set diagonally on a 3¼ × 3¼ inches square of ½-inch plywood painted with the same dark green enamel which I used for the inside of the egg.

The second toothpick holder is presided over by a white doggie. The chicken egg was strengthened with gesso and cut with the Dremel, leaving about two-thirds of the shell. The interior was coated with

Black Jewel Box, a perfect gift for a man.

liquid solder and painted with black enamel.

The exterior was decoupaged with pink roses. For additional strength the rim was set with two rows of straw braid, both inside and out and the braid was given three coats of transparent enamel. The egg was set in a roller bearing painted with white enamel.

The base for this egg also measures 3¼ × 3¼ and was left in its natural wood tone but given three coats of transparent enamel. I would not submerge either of these holders in water, but they can easily be wiped clean from time to time with a damp cloth.

The Black Jewel Box

This large goose egg decorated entirely in black, gold and pearls is another example of striking simplicity. I began with an egg 7¼ inches in diameter and bisected it vertically in half. After cutting and washing, I hinged it in the exact center.

It was then given four coats of black celluloid enamel which produces a lustrous black finish. The interior of the egg was painted with Liquid Gold Leaf. The upper half of the exterior shell was given a row of gold cord, followed by a row of white pearls and the pearls were framed by a second row of gold cord.

The finial was a gold-colored binding in the center of which I placed a large white pearl. The binding was given a row of small white pearls at the jointure.

The lower half of the egg was simply finished with one row of gold cord at the very edge.

The base is a small round plaque of poplar wood (available in craft stores) on which I placed a 1½-inch gold plastic curtain ring, surrounded by a strand of white pearls. The base is painted black.

In the center of the ring is a black-enameled metal aerosol cap on which the egg rests.

I particularly like this method of forming a base for a jewel case. The round plaque is pleasing to the eye and in harmony with the roundness of the egg. The base also has great stability—I do not like bases that tip easily.

This design, almost austere in its simplicity, would look well almost anywhere. There is, however, no reason why it could not be made up in any color that would fit well into your plan of decoration for a particular room.

It need not even be used for a jewel case. It is so beautifully simple that it would make an excellent gift for a man and can be used to hold matches or cuff links.

Lining the Jewel Box

The interior of the jewel-box design may be finished any way you like. A simple drapery of silk, white or colored is always effective. For a striking color contrast I lined one of these boxes in brilliant orange.

Using a flexible tape measure, cut a piece of soft silk just long enough to go around the inside of the egg, allowing for seaming. Glue this just around the edge of the shell, allowing the folds of the silk to fall in their own natural, graceful drape. (The silk should be wide enough, 3 to 3½ inches, to extend to the bottom of the egg.)

Cut a small, rounded, slightly oblong piece of cardboard. Measure to be sure it will fit nicely in the bottom of the egg. Cover cardboard with silk, pulling it taut on the underside and gluing down firmly. Weight until dry so the piece will be perfectly flat.

The interior top rim of the shell may be finished with gold cord or flat braid.

Cover top part of shell interior in the same manner as the bottom part.

Velvet may also be used for linings. Velvet is heavier and will take up more room but makes such a lovely and durable lining that I sometimes like to use it.

Cinderella Coach, a marvelous topping for a birthday cake.

Measure as before. You can avoid some of the "bunchiness" by making tiny box pleats in the velvet at each end of the egg. Make a little platform for the bottom as you did with the silk.

If you would like to put a tiny chain on the interior to regulate the distance that the egg may be opened and closed, be sure to secure this before you put in the lining.

Lining eggs is not difficult once you "get the hang of it." As with so many other things it just takes a little practice and experimentation with different materials. Brocade, if not too stiff, makes a lovely lining; even leather can be used.

Perhaps the easiest finish of all for interiors is simply to paint them with gold, silver, or copper Liquid Leaf or a waterproof celluloid enamel in a harmonizing or contrasting color.

The Cinderella Coach

This exquisitely detailed gold plastic coach is obtainable at a supply house for cake decorations as are the two tiny figurines used for Cinderella and the Prince.

Since the goose egg I was working with was too tall to fit well in the coach I cut a small portion off of the small end of the egg and glued a piece of cardboard to it in the manner described in the chapter "Eggs on the Half Shell." The rest of the egg was cut with the opening in the curved heart shape and covered with ruby-red velvet, outlined with gold braid and pearls.

I made a flat pillow of red velvet to cover the cardboard and allowed this to extend forward about ½-inch. Cinderella was positioned on this pillow.

After removing the plastic liner (this slips off easily) that comes with the coach, I positioned the egg in the exact center of the coach so that it should show through the oval-shaped aperture.

Two tiny scraps of red velvet were also placed on the coach to unify the design and add a bit more color. The tiny Prince stands outside the coach.

This coach egg would be adorable for a birthday cake for a young girl —it is one of the simplest and easy-to-make designs in this book.

If you make this for a particular young lady and know her favorite color, use that instead of the red velvet. The gold of the coach will harmonize well with just about any color of the rainbow.

The "Great Pumpkin" Planter

This is one of the fun things I enjoyed making the most. And it is so utterly simple that you could turn them out by the dozen. Many pumpkins are of a rounded oblong shape and that is what this egg resembles after being painted (three coats) with brilliant orange waterproof celluloid enamel.

To waterproof the interior I gave it a coating of liquid solder (craft steel may also be used) and allowed this to dry thoroughly before painting it with waterproof celluloid black enamel.

The simple band of gold loop braid which decorates the edge was sprayed with clear lacquer before it was placed on the egg.

The attractive gold base was purchased at a department store and was originally designed to hold a bottle of nail polish. I removed the finger rest but retained the delightful little seahorse.

Since the egg was fully waterproofed, it may be used to hold either natural or artificial flowers. You might even grow a small plant in it such as a tiny portion of sweet potato eye which will make a graceful trailing vine, or one of the very small species of ivy. The orange color

This eggshell vase can easily be made waterproof.

of the planter makes a very attractive background for any type of small greenery.

This type of treatment will work well for a larger egg, such as an ostrich egg, if you decide you would like one for a planter.

Though I have put my planter egg on a stand, there is no reason why it could not be hung or suspended in any manner you choose. Simply make a suitable harness of string, leather, ribbon, chain, etc. and place the egg inside it.

If you have the room, you could even put a tree branch in a small flower pot and hang several of these planters from it, each one with a small bit of greenery growing inside.

The Water Sprite

This is made with a large goose egg, bisected in half vertically and hinged at the largest end of the egg. The interior of the egg was painted with rose-pink enamel in a deep shade. When dry, this was coated with

Water Sprite egg, displayed on decorated driftwood.

transparent adhesive and covered with ballantine—resulting in a shell pink.

The interior edge has one row of narrow gold cord as its only decoration. An amusing winged water sprite sits in the shell.

The exterior of the shell was given five coats of metallic model paint (Pactra) in Burgundy red. This paint gives back such a beautiful finish by itself that I added just one row of gold cord and a row of pearls around the exterior rim. Here, again, simplicity of design is very effective.

The base is an interesting piece of chunky driftwood which I picked up on the beach of Lake Texoma. It is weather- and water-worn and has an unusual pattern varying from cream color to almost black. Small, shallow channels have been carved into it by some form of marine life.

Into these small channels I glued pearls of various sizes, singly and

Lemon eggs, an interesting centerpiece for the table.

in groups, looking as if they spilled from the shell and scattered at random.

No two pieces of driftwood are ever alike, but when you are searching for bases or backgrounds for your shells look for pieces with interesting shapes and textures.

Also look for small, decorative shells which may be placed on the wood along with the pearls to add to the marine look. Mermaids or a small Neptune placed in the eggshell also make for an interesting effect as do figurines. Or you may simply use a small heap of pearls or some of the chocolate-covered gold coins, or both together. If you heap up the pearls, glue them together with transparent jewelry cement. Even a tiny pirate ship inside the shell would be attractive.

You may like to place this ornament on a round mirror and use it for a centerpiece for your table—nice, especially in summer.

Lemon Eggs ... Plus Yellow Daisies

This makes an interesting centerpiece for your dining room table at any season of the year or use it in your living room for that bare spot that needs a bit of extra perking up—it will do a great deal to lighten a dark corner.

The best eggs to use for this are the small size. (In a later chapter I will explain about egg quality and egg size.)

You can remove the egg contents easily from one end only by using the little rubber and plastic device described in an earlier chapter. If you insert the plastic tube in the small end of the egg the "insides" will blow out more easily. Rinse well with water which you can shake out—or blow out if you prefer.

Since a small residue of water often remains in the egg I always set them upright, hole downward, in a discarded egg carton to drain for an hour or so before painting.

Using a 1/4-inch-wide flat brush, paint each egg with three coats of yellow celluloid enamel. Allow 15 minutes to half an hour between coats depending on whether the day is dry or humid. Make the coats thin so you will not have a buildup.

Slip the egg on a drying rack to hold it upright between coats.

Cover pieces of wire with green florist tape, making a tiny ball on the end through which you will push the hole in the egg. Do this carefully so you will not penetrate the shell at the far end. Wrap another small piece of tape around the wire just outside the egg.

The basket may be of any type, but I like this arrangement best in a basket without a handle. Pack the basket with excelsior or a piece of Styrofoam cut to fit. Obtain one or two bunches of artificial yellow daisies.

Insert the wires holding the eggs in the Styrofoam and put the daisies in between the eggs. Pack eggs and daisies together solidly so the arrangement will remain in place.

Découpage a Purse with Eggshells

This purse is truly "different" and one that any eager "egger" would be proud to carry for all the world to see and admire as a symbol of her craft.

And, unlike the other purse described in the chapter on eggshelling, this one may be made with a gable top or curved sides. This is a very personal fun thing, for it will also have your initials on it.

Start this elegant project by selecting a wooden purse of good quality. It does not matter whether it is walnut, cherry, maple or good white pine, but try to avoid open-grained woods.

Check the purse over carefully. Flaws in the wood, unless deep, will not matter, but be sure all the corners are well glued. Try to visualize how the purse will look when the hardware is on it. Consider the size: If you plan to make this purse as a present for a child—and children love these—choose one of the smaller ones.

With this method of decorating we work only on a small area at a time so curved sides or tops can be handled easily.

Begin by brushing white glue on a small area of the box, about the size of a 50-cent piece. Now, take a small piece of eggshell—and here again you can use your broken shells—and push it down on the glue with your fingertip. The rounded shell will crack under the slight pressure of your finger and embed itself naturally in the glue. Continue working in this manner until the entire surface of the purse is covered.

After the purse is covered and well dried, take a flat brush and go over the entire surface with two successive coats of white glue that has been slightly diluted with water. Dry well between coats.

If you plan to give the purse a white background, as I did, follow this with two coats of gesso. If you want to give the purse a colored background paint with two coats of acrylic in the planned color.

The gesso or acrylic should be followed by two coats of water lacquer (Deep Flex is a good brand.) Let dry between coats.

Antique by rubbing with black tempera paint, brushing on and wiping off with a soft cloth.

You will have an irregular surface with high and low places. If you feel you want more of the black to show in the crevices, you may put on a second coat, repeating as before.

After the antiquing is dry, finish by spraying on two coats of high gloss crystal-clear instant-finish decoupage spray.

The purse hardware, obtainable at any craft shop, should match or harmonize with the color of the purse. I chose a black and white plastic handle and "gold" hinge, clasp and ball feet.

My initials "L R H" add a very personal touch and these, too, are readily obtainable. The ones I found were backed with adhesive which did not adhere too well to the slick surface of the purse. I scraped the adhesive off carefully and glued them into position with contact adhesive and I have had no further difficulty.

This purse is very versatile and attractive in many colors, but it is especially smashing if made up in brown and antiqued with black. This combination of colors has the expensive look of alligator and may be attained for a fraction of the cost.

I lined my purse with black felt, top and bottom, and ran a row of ½-inch braid (flat) around the edge. This is easy to do. Measure the interior around the top and then the depth. Cut in one long strip to exact size. Try for fit and cut off any excess. Glue down with white glue. Measure interior bottom and cut felt to fit. Repeat with top of purse. Glue on braid.

Fine-Feathered Egg

What could possibly be more appropriate than covering an egg with feathers? And when these feathers are so exquisitely beautiful as those of the pheasant, these unusual eggs become even more interesting and attractive.

This is one of the easiest types of egg decoration but does take a little time and patience. Again, I would suggest, as I have so often done before, that you decorate several eggs at a time.

Begin at the smallest end of the egg (chicken, duck, goose, turkey, or smaller eggs if you like—very small eggs are impractical). Feathers have a natural curve and, after cutting off about ⅓ to ¼ of the shaft, depending on the size of the feathers I am working with, I glue the first feathers down so they will cover the end of the egg as they follow their natural bend.

While the first egg is drying I take up another and proceed in the same way, perhaps doing three or four before I go back to the first one.

The next layer of feathers is laid on all around the egg as before, letting about ½ to ⅓ of the first layer show. Continue in this manner, just as if you were laying shingles on a roof. Let each layer dry well before putting on the next one. As you approach the other end of the egg you will find that you need to cut the layers of feathers progressively shorter.

For the very last layer of feathers, I used small pieces of nicely curving feathers only about ¾ of an inch long.

Last spring, after a particularly heavy rain and windstorm, I found a bird's nest under one of my big hackberry trees and decided to save it. After letting it dry thoroughly, I sprayed it with insecticide and put it away in a box.

When I had completed my fine-feathered egg I put it in this nest and felt it looked right at home.

CHAPTER SIXTEEN

The Insides of the Eggs

Obviously, if you get carried away with decorating the outsides of the eggs, you are going to have a lot of insides to dispose of in some manner, and if you are as thrifty as I am you will not want to waste even one egg.

You don't have to develop a mania that leads in only one direction—scrambled eggs. Now there is nothing wrong with scrambled eggs, an occasional serving is just fine, but my family is apt to rebel if they get them too often. Nevertheless, since just about everybody seems to think this is the smart thing to do, let's start with a good recipe:

> 4 eggs
> 1 tablespoon cooking oil
> 1/4 to 1/2 cup milk
> salt and pepper to taste

Beat eggs, add liquid and spices. Warm oil in frying pan over low heat. Add slightly beaten egg mixture.

Let eggs cook until mixture begins to thicken around the bottom and edges.

Lift the masses of egg mixture from edges toward center, scraping egg from bottom of pan. Repeat until entire mixture is of creamy consistency.

Serve immediately. The mixture will continue to cook if left in hot pan.

Here's another good way to use eggs:

Fluffy Omelet

4 eggs
¼ cup water
½ teaspoon salt
⅛ teaspoon pepper
1 teaspoon dill seed (optional)
1 tablespoon cooking oil

Separate the white from the yolk. (This is a recipe I use when I cut out a portion of the shell for a window egg and separation is easy.)

Add liquid and salt and pepper to egg yolks, beat until thick and lemon-colored.

Beat egg white until stiff but not dry.

Fold egg-yolk mixture into egg whites until well blended. Add dill seed.

Heat omelet pan, add oil and be sure sides and bottom of pan are well covered with oil. Remove from direct heat.

Turn mixture into pan and spread evenly. Place over low heat and cook slowly. Turn occasionally to brown omelet evenly.

French Toast

4 eggs, beaten
⅔ cup milk
¼ teaspoon salt
12 slices bread
2 tablespoons cooking oil or fat
Cinnamon and sugar, mixed

Combine eggs, milk and salt.

Dip each side of bread in egg mixture.

Brown on both sides in the fat or oil on a hot griddle—3 to 4 minutes on each side.

Sprinkle with cinnamon and serve immediately.

Indian Corn Pudding

1 tablespoon butter or margarine
1 tablespoon flour
1 cup scalded milk
1 teaspoon salt
⅛ teaspoon pepper
1 teaspoon sugar
16 oz. can cream style corn or
    10 oz. package frozen whole kernel
4 eggs, slightly beaten

Preheat oven to 375° F. (moderate).
Oil one quart casserole.
Melt butter or margarine and blend in flour.
Add milk, salt, pepper and sugar.
Add corn and heat slightly.
Blend eggs into corn mixture.
Pour into casserole and place casserole in pan of hot water.
Bake one hour or until set.

Eggs Oriental

Sauce

1 cup chicken broth
2 tablespoons soy sauce

1 tablespoon cornstarch
¼ cup water

Egg Mixture

6 eggs
1½ cups pork, cooked and diced
⅔ cup onions, small, thinly sliced or slice fresh green onions

16-ounce can bean sprouts, drained
4-ounce can mushrooms, drained
2 tablespoons cooking oil

Combine broth and soy sauce.
Heat to boiling.
Blend cornstarch and water.
Stir slowly into broth.
Cook and stir constantly until thickened.
Keep warm while cooking egg mixture.
Beat eggs until very thick and light.
Fold in the pork, onions, bean sprouts and mushrooms.
Heat oil in frypan over moderate heat.
Pour the egg mixture by ½ cupfuls into the pan.
Cook until lightly browned on one side, turn and brown the other side.
Serve the sauce over the patties.

Cowboy Sandwich

6 slices bacon (dice before cooking
3 tablespoons minced onion
6 eggs, beaten
¼ cup milk
¼ teaspoon salt
⅛ teaspoon pepper
¼ teaspoon tabasco sauce (optional)
4 tablespoons margarine (or butter)
12 slices bread

Partially fry diced bacon.
Add minced onion; cook until just clear and transparent.
Mix eggs with milk and seasonings (including tabasco).
Pour over bacon and onion.
Fry on one side until brown.
Turn, fry on other side, cut into six pieces.
Butter slices of bread.
Put egg filling on six slices of bread; cover with the other six slices.
Makes 6 sandwiches.

All of these egg recipes are just great for luncheon or a main dish and, while the recipes call for chicken eggs, there is no reason why they cannot be adapted to turkey, goose or duck eggs—in the case of the larger goose eggs use one less than the directions call for.

Versatile eggs may also be used as the basis for a number of delicious desserts. How about making some of them up into cream puffs and eclairs. Don't let those fancy names frighten you—there is nothing more easily made. Here's how:

Cream Puffs

1 cup sifted flour (all purpose)
½ cup butter or shortening
¼ teaspoon salt
1 cup water
4 or 5 eggs (depending on whether large or small)

Sift flour, measure and sift again.
Combine butter or shortening, salt and water in saucepan.
Bring to boil and remove from heat.
Add flour all at once.
Beat until dough leaves sides of pan and cooks slightly.
Add eggs one at a time. (Eggs should be at room temperature.)
Beat until batter is smooth after each addition.
Drop by heaping tablespoonfuls on greased (or teflon) cookie sheet.

Bake in hot oven (450° F.) about 20 minutes, reduce temperature to moderate oven (350°) and continue baking another 20 minutes or until thoroughly dry and holding their shape. Makes 12 large or 24 small puffs.

Make eclairs the same way but shape the dough into logs before baking.

Chocolate Filling for Puffs

4 ounces chocolate (unsweetened)
1½ cups sugar
2 tablespoons flour
3 cups milk
6 egg yolks, slightly beaten
1 teaspoon vanilla

Melt chocolate in a heavy saucepan over very low heat.

Blend in sugar, flour, and enough milk to make a thick, smooth texture.

Gradually blend in remaining milk.

Cook over low heat, stirring constantly, until mixture thickens slightly.

Stir a little of the hot mixture into the egg yolks. Then stir the egg yolk mixture into the hot mixture.

Cook a few minutes more over very low heat, stirring constantly until thickened.

Add vanilla and stir.

Cover until used, to keep surface from forming a film. May be used warm or chilled as filling for puffs.

Hawaiian Pineapple Freeze

1 cup vanilla cookie crumbs
2 tablespoons butter or margarine (melted)
1 cup whipping cream
3 eggs
⅛ teaspoon salt
⅔ cup sugar
¼ cup lemon juice
1 small can crushed pineapple

Mix ⅔ cup cookie crumbs with margarine; spread in an 8-inch-square pan. Chill.

Chill whipping cream.

Beat eggs.
Add salt, sugar, lemon juice and pineapple to eggs.
Cook over hot water until thick, stirring constantly. Cool.
Whip the cream.
Fold whipped cream into egg mixture.
Pour egg mixture over crumb crust.
Top with remaining crumbs.
Freeze.

What do you know about egg grades? A bit of study here may help you to decide how you can best purchase eggs for decorative purposes (the shells, that is) and still make good use of the egg contents.

Generally (where chicken eggs are used), I recommend that eggs used for decoration should be the largest, whitest eggs you can find—but not always—for brown eggs can be attractive for certain techniques. And for the "Lemon Eggs With Yellow Daisies," or the Fruit and Flower pictures, the small-sized eggs may work out better.

Here are some pointers about eggs:

Size refers to minimum weight per dozen.

Size may be shown within the grade shield or elsewhere on the carton.

Size and quality are not related—they are entirely different.

For example, large eggs may be of high or low quality; high-quality eggs may be either large or small.

The sizes most often found are:

	Minimum weight per dozen
Extra Large	27 oz.
Large	24 oz.
Medium	21 oz.

Other sizes sometimes available are:

Jumbo	30 oz.
Small	18 oz.
Peewee	15 oz.

Here is how grade (quality) is decided:

Grade refers to interior quality and condition and appearance of shell.

Aqua-blue duck egg in the middle foreground shows the size of duck eggs compared to chicken egg beside it.

Grade AA (or fresh fancy). This egg covers a small area, the white is thick and stands high, the yolk is firm and high.

Grade A. This egg covers a moderate area, the white is reasonably thick and stands fairly high, the yolk is firm and high.

Grade B eggs (apt to be a bit runny and yolk may not hold up well when egg is broken) still good for general cooking and baking where appearance is not important.

If you plan to decorate eggs in quantity this classification may assist you in purchasing, for usually eggs are priced according to their grade and size.

What I am discussing here is, of course, chicken eggs. Duck, goose, and turkey eggs, etc. may also be judged by similar standards for freshness and quality when you extract the contents. You will be the best judge as to their freshness and whether or not you wish to use them for food.

So much for using the insides of the eggs for cooking. Actually I find it downright comforting, and revel in the knowledge that I don't have to *eat* them all!

Maybe there's nothing glamorous about egg on the face of it, but considering that it was good enough for Cleopatra, maybe it bears looking into.

Let's face the hard-boiled facts—our ancestors lived closer to nature than we do today and they learned to make use of her gifts for beauty and health. And that's just what a growing number of naturalists and beauty enthusiasts are advocating today—egging us on—in beauty's name, to give the egg a try.

History records that even the early Christians of ancient Rome used facial masks made of eggs, just as kitchen cosmeticians are urging us to try today. Egg masks were popular with Marie Antoinette and her court ladies; they were still popular in the time of Queen Victoria (who was very attractive in her youth with a lovely, unblemished skin, for which English women are famous) and today they are becoming popular again as a home treatment.

So, while you are beautifying the eggs, it might be fun to take a beauty treatment yourself. Eggs cleanse, soften, tone and tighten pores. They're also chemical-free, inexpensive (you have them anyway), and as near as your local grocery store or supermarket. Eggs are the same today as they were thousands of years ago, unchanged and unchanging, and they can be just as beneficial today as they were in the times of the great beauty queens.

There are numerous recipes for egg masks, some purportedly concocted long ago by the ancient Babylonians who mixed a small quantity of dry herb powder with three whole eggs. They believed this mixture would improve the circulation as well as cleanse the skin.

Here is another suggestion: wash your face with a mild soap and warm water. Pat dry. After beating the white of one raw egg until stiff, add one teaspoon of honey or lemon, mixing in well. Now, with a pad of absorbent cotton or your fingers, smooth the mixture over your entire face. Allow to remain for 15 minutes. Rinse, using warm water and a soft cloth to remove all traces. Splash cool water on your face and pat dry. It will make you feel refreshed.

It is said that a famous queen and her ladies used to beat 3 or 4 egg whites together with one grain of camphor and one of alum (both famous home remedies for shrinking large pores and clearing blemishes) until stiff. This fluffy mixture should be spread over your face (and don't forget your neck and arms) and allowed to dry for about an hour. Rinse off with warm water followed by cool.

Egg masks are particularly good for tired, oily, dry, or blemished skin.

Those who have oily skin particularly swear by a mask of simple, raw beaten egg white, left on for 10 to 15 minutes. On the other hand, if your skin is too dry, you might try adding olive oil to egg yolk, making a mask of this to see if it will correct the problem.

An oily skin treatment which is a bit more complicated but often very effective combines egg whites, oatmeal and honey. This should be thoroughly mixed into a smooth paste and gently massaged into the skin for five to ten minutes.

Have you considered your elbows lately? If they are unsightly, beat up an egg white with a little milk of magnesia and cover them with a thick paste of this mixture. Leave on for a few hours and then wash off paste with lemon juice.

While you are busy decorating the eggs, why not use some of the insides to give yourself a beauty treatment, too? You and your face are just going to be sitting there working anyway and a mask won't interfere one bit. And think of the satisfaction of having both you and the eggs emerge looking prettier.

And what about your hair? Eggs can help here, too. Suppose it is brittle, dull, thin, or generally lifeless. Eggs can come to the rescue.

Lightly beat the yolk of one egg and thoroughly rub into the scalp, massaging as you go and using the egg instead of a shampoo. I can very well remember that my father as well as my mother used to do this and they both possessed beautiful, thick, luxuriant hair. Unlike many of his contemporaries, my father never became bald. My father's hair was blond and my mother's raven black—turning to white and silver respectively as they both grew older. Only the color changed—the life, texture and body remained the same throughout their lives.

Even your eyebrows can benefit from a special egg shampoo. Just rub a teaspoonful of the well-beaten egg into the hair roots, leave it on a few minutes, rinse off and shape them by brushing. They will benefit just as much as the hair on your head.

So, whether you use your egg insides for cooking, facial masks, or shampoos, none of them need ever be wasted or thrown away. If they are still in useful condition, you will find they are good for some purpose.

And that's a hard-boiled fact!

It's been fun traveling down the trail with you. We've glorified a lot of eggs, visited the chuck wagon and peeked into the beauty bar together. I've enjoyed every minute of it and hope you have, too. Good luck and good eggin'.

Suppliers

Baby Dolls (Papoose)

Maid of Scandinavia, 3245 Raleigh Avenue, Minneapolis, Minnesota 55416
Wilton Enterprises, Inc., 833 West 115th Street, Chicago, Illinois 60643

Beading Supplies

Indian City, U.S.A., Anadarko, Oklahoma, 73005
Mrs. E. M. Roberts, Beading Supplies, 211 West Broadway, Anadarko, Oklahoma 73005
McKee's Indian Store, 122 N.W. First Street, Anadarko, Oklahoma 73005
Lee Wards, Elgin, Illinois 60120

Colors, Paints, and Finishes

Herter's Inc. Rural Route 1, Waseca, Minnesota 56093
  (Celluloid enamel, Luminous paint, Flitters, and Swiss Metallics)
Maid of Scandinavia, 3245 Raleigh Avenue, Minneapolis, Minnesota 55416.
  (Ukranian Easter Egg Kit)

Egg Suppliers

C & R Duck Farm, Westhampton, L.I., New York. Duck eggs only, regular and double yolk.
Herb Allen's Hole In One, 3926 Kenosha Ave., San Diego, California 92117. Clean blown goose eggs. Has method of blowing eggs with single mini hole.
Hoffman Goose Hatchery, Gratz, Pennsylvania 17030. Goose eggs may be ordered whole in season (up to about May), or blown (2 holes), out of season. Also has aqua-blue duck eggs, turkey eggs and swan eggs.
Hockman's, Box 7187, San Diego, California 92107. Goose eggs, Emden and Toulouse only.
Rock Mountain Farm, Box 167, Mosier, Oregon 97049. Quail, banty, blue duck, regular duck, goose finch, canary, bobwhite quail, pigeon, ringneck pheasant, common parakeet, guinea, peafowl, dove, redleg partridge, tinnamou.
Schlitz Goose Egg Hatchery and Breeding Farm, Bancroft, Iowa 50517. Goose eggs only.

Leather

Tandy Leather Company (120 stores nationwide)
  For Omega and Cova dye, dyeing supplies, brushes, leather and leather craft tools. Plastic gloves and beads.

Tools

Dremel Moto-Tool—Model 261 is easiest for a woman to use—made by Dremel Manufacturing Company, P.O. Box 518, Racine, Wisconsin 53401

Trims

A & L Hobbicraft, Inc., 50 Broadway, P.O. Box 7025, Asheville, North Carolina 28807. Braids, Brayer (hard rubber roller for use with block-printing inks), baskets, beads, block-printing inks, drawing inks, frames, gesso, jewelry findings, modeling paste, plaques, purses (wooden for decorating), paint (acrylics and watercolors).

Boutique Trims, South Lyon, Michigan 48178. Balls, ballantine, beads, bell caps, braids, cameos, chain, diamond dust, egg stands, flowers, metal findings, metal filigrees, jewelry findings, jump rings, lace, Moto-Tool No. 260 (tool only or kit with attachments), miniatures, pearl strands, rhinestones, sequins, tassels, velvet ribbon.

Brandon Memorabilia, Inc., 3 West 30th Street, New York, New York 10001. Gold motifs, gold medallions, lithographed pictures, miniatures.

Carpet & Remnant Shop, 721 N. Commerce, Ardmore, Oklahoma 73401. Fake fur, sequins.

Dremel Manufacturing Company, P.O. Box 518, Racine, Wisconsin 53401. Manufacturers of Dremel Moto-Tool No. 260 (generic name for Moto-Tool, "rotary grinding tool").

Grieger's, Inc., 1633 East Walnut St., Pasadena, California 91109. Cameos, gems and gemstones, jewelry stones, jump rings, metal chain, plastic chain, rhinestones.

Herter's, Inc., Rural Route 1, Waseca, Minnesota 56093. Celluloid enamel, French Flitters (trade name for ballantine), luminous paint, pearl lacquer, pheasant feathers, Swiss metallics (silver and gold).

Indian City, U.S.A., Anadarko, Oklahoma 73005. Beads and beading supplies.

Jack Krentz Ceramics, 1300 Bixby, Ardmore, Oklahoma 73401. Ceramic egg stands.

Lee Wards, Elgin, Illinois 60120. Braid, bell caps, beads, one-loop oval cages, feathers, felt, flowers, sequins, velvet ribbon.

Maid of Scandinavia, 3245 Raleigh Ave., Minneapolis, Minnesota 55416. Baby dolls (papoose and cradle dolls), chenille bees, Cinderella coach, harlequin trims, icing trims, miniature champagne glasses (Chapter III—bases for eggheads), tiny plastic birds and other miniatures. Ukranian Easter Egg kit.

McKees' Indian Store, 122 N.W. First St., Anadarko, Oklahoma 73005. Beads and beading supplies.

Parks Flower Book, Greenwood, South Carolina 29646. Gazania Sunshine hybrids, African daisy, etc.

Reynolds, Mrs. E. M., 211 W. Broadway, Anadarko, Oklahoma 73005. Beads and beading supplies.

Tandy Leather Company, 141 Medallion Center, Dallas, Texas 75214. (Tandy has stores nationwide.) Beads, beading supplies, Cova and Omega dyes, brushes, swabs, leather and leathercraft tools.

Thieves Market, 118 A St. N.W., Ardmore, Oklahoma 73401. Braid, butterflies (real wings, cardboard bodies), eggshell finish decoupage, gold leaf (base and adhesive), Hyplar matte medium and varnish, Liquid Leaf (gold, silver, etc.), miniatures, pearls, Patricia Nimrock's Plastic Spray, signs of the Zodiac, pearl lacquer, poplar wood plaques, wooden purses. Liquid lead and liquid steel.

Webb Office Supply, 30 N. Washington, Ardmore, Oklahoma 73401. Acrylic paint, paint brushes, fluorescent paint, India ink, tube watercolors.

Miscellaneous

Jewelry stones used on brocade appliqué eggs—Grieger's, Inc., 1633 West Walnut Street, Pasadena, California 91109

Bees, cake stands (swan)—Maid of Scandinavia, 3245 Raleigh Avenue, Minneapolis, Minnesota 55416

Eggshell Marker—The Egg Shell, Box F, South Lyon, Michigan 48178

Index

Acrylic paint, 94-95
Alexandra, Empress, xi
Anemone (symbol), 27
Anemone pulsatilla (Pasque flower), 5-6
Angelfish eggs, 77-80
Appliqué technique, 113-115
Aquarius, the Waterman, 38
Aries, the Ram, 38-39

Baby in bassinet, 89-92
Beehive eggs, 116-117
Belgium, xiii
Bell (Easter symbol), 26
Bird symbols, 26
Braid trims, 98, 102
Brandon Memorabilia, Inc., 119
Bulgaria, xiv
Bullock cart design, 149-150
Butterfly (symbol), 27
Butterfly egg, 31-32

Cameos, 31
Cancer, the Crab, 39
Candy eggs, xii
Capricorn, the Goat, 40
China, xii
Chocolate eggs, xii
Chocolate Filling for Puffs (recipe), 165
Christian festivals, xii
Christmas, ix, xi, 35, 97, 99, 120

Cinderella coach, 153-154
Colors, 93-102
    egg stand and, 103
    natural egg, 94
    paints and finishes, 94-102
    strength of, 93
Copper braid, 21
Council of Nicea, xiii
Cove Dye Remover, 57-58
Cowboy Sandwich (recipe), 164
Crisco, 5
Cream Puffs (recipe), 164-165
    Chocolate Filling for, 165
Crucifixion, 26, 27
Cutting process:
    emptying egg contents for, 72, 74
    glueing and drying, 74-75
    goose eggs, 70-72
    hinge size and, 75
    how to begin, 69-70
    to join half shells, 75
    tools, 69, 70-71
Czechoslovakia, 27

Découpaging, 124-125
    purse with eggshells, 156-160
Donkey (symbol), 26
Dremel Moto-Tool, 69, 70-71, 141
Eagle (symbol), 26
Easter, ix, xi, xii-xiv, 97, 120
    customs connected with, xiii-xiv

  date of, xiii
  symbols, xii, xiv, 26-28
Easter Egg dye, 127
Easter rabbit, xii, 2
Egg masks, 168-169
Egg molds, xii
Egg shampoo, 169
Egg stands:
  antique look, 104-105
  and Christmas tree display, 106-107
  coordinating color with, 103
  how to make, 103-107
Egg tree, 23-35
  braid and bell cap, 24-25
  buttons and jewelry stones, 30-35
  candies, 35
  Easter symbols, 26-28
  edible possibilities, 35
  how to make, 23-26
  marbles, 30-31
  ornament at the bottom, 24-26
  sequins, 28-30
Eggheads, ix-x, 43-52
  bride and groom, 52
  drawing and painting face, 44
  Easter bunny, 47-48
  French lady, 46-47
  funny face, 48-49
  Halloween witch, 45-46
  leprechaun, 50
  materials, 43
  Santa Claus, 46
  Three Kings, 50-51
  Undine the water nymph, 44
Eggs Oriental (recipe), 163
Eggshells:
  covering objects with, 127-136
  cutting, 69-75
  découpaging a purse with, 156-160
Egypt (ancient), xi
Eierlesen (contest), xiii
Enamel finish, 95
Enamel paint, 97
England, xii, 5
Eostre (goddess of spring), xiii
Ethiopians, xiii

Fabergé, Peter Carl, xi
Festique Spangle Copper, 21
Fine-feathered egg, 160
Finishes, 93-102
  braid trim, 98, 102
  easy-to-make drying rack, 97-98
  enamel, 95
  for German scrap, 124-125
  gloss, 95
  golf-leaf, 30, 98-99
  with metallics, 96, 99
  translucent (flitters), 96
Finland, xiv
Fixatives, 97
Flitters, 96
Flower symbols of Easter, 27-28

Flowers and ferns, 9-16
    best time to pick, 10
    coloring the egg, 12-13
    drying medium, 10-12
    drying the petals, 14
    eggshell preparation, 12
    finishing touches, 15-16
    removing egg contents, 13-14
Fluffy Omelet (recipe), 162
Football eggs, 115-116
France, xiii
French Toast (recipe), 162
Fruit and flower plaque, 137-139

"Gem Stones of the United States," 34
Gemini, the Twins, 39
Geological Survey Bulletin, 34
German scrap:
    cutting, 120-121
    decorating with, 119-125
    finishes, 124-125
    gluing on, 122-123
Germany, xii, xiii, 1
Gloss finish, 95
Gold braid trim, 98, 102
Gold leaf, 30, 98-99
Good Friday, xiii
Goose eggs:
    cutting, 70-72
    sources of supply, 74
Grades (eggs), 166-167
Great Pumpkin planter, 154-155
Greece, xiv
Greece (ancient), xi
Grieger's, Inc., 20-21

Half shell, the, 77-92
    angelfish eggs, 77-80
    baby in bassinet, 89-92
    lavabo design, 83-89
    leather and horse brasses, 82-83
    on velvet band, 80-82
Halloween, ix, 35, 45
Hawaiian Pineapple Freeze (recipe), 165-166
Hayes, Rutherford B., xiv
Herter's Celluloid Enamel, 15
Herter's French Flitters, 96
Herter's Pearl Laquer, 15, 22
Herter's Swiss Metallics, 96
Holy Saturday, xiv
Holy Week, xiv

Hopi Indians, 62-64
Horse brasses, leather and, 82-83
Hungary, xiv
Hyplar Matte Medium & Varnish, 16
Indian Corn Pudding (recipe), 162-163
Indian Cradle, 53-56
    clothing the papoose, 56
Insides, using, 161-169
    for cooking, 161-166
    for facial treatment, 167-169
Ireland, xiii
Italy, xiii-xiv

Jewel box, 151-153
    lining, 152-153
Jeweled eggs:
    for all occasions, 23-35
    of the Zodiac, 37-42
Jewelry stones, 18-20, 21

Kachina doll, 62-64

Lacquer paint, how to apply, 99
Lavabo design, 83-89
Leather, and horse brasses, 82-83
Lemon eggs (plus yellow daisies), 156
Leo, the Lion, 39
Libra, the Scales, 39
Lion (symbol), 26
Luminous paint, 95-96

Marie, Dowager Empress, xi
Maundy Thursday, xiii, 26
Mesopotamia, xii
Metallic glitter, 96, 99
Metallic sequins, 97
Metallic spray paints, 97
Mexico, xiv, 8, 27
Mushroom with silver fringe, 139-140

Natural materials, use of, 1-16
Natural Materials, 1-16
    onion skin broth, 1-5, 6
    flowers and ferns, 9-16
Netherlands, xiv
New Year, festival of (spring equinox), xii

Omega Dye, 57

Onion skin broth, 1-5, 6
    cooking the eggs, 4
    removing the wrappings, 4-5
    room display ideas, 7-8
    room temperature and, 4, 6
    rubbing with cooking oil, 5
    wrapping procedure, 2-4, 5
Oriental pieces, 143-145

Paints, 93-102
    acrylic, 94-95
    enamel, 97
    luminous, 95-96
Passover, xiii
Paste colors, 127
Persia (ancient), xi
Phoenix, the, 26
Piñatas, xiv
Pisces, the Fish, 38
Poland, 101
Pueblo Indians, 62-64
Puerto Rico, 27
Purses, 134-135
    découpaging with eggshells, 158-160
    enamel trim, 135

Recipes, 161-169
    for cooking, 161-166
    for egg masks, 168
Resurrection, xii, 26, 27
Rhinestones, 21, 98, 114
Rit or Putnam dye, 6
Rome (ancient), xi
Rose beads, 18-21
Rose-scented eggs, 17-22
    applying the finish, 21-22
    copper braid, 21
    gold-colored, 21
    grinding process, 18
    jewelry stones, 18-20, 21
    making in quantity, 22
    picking the petals, 17-18
    rhinestone, 21
    silver-colored, 21
Rumania, xiv
Russia, xi, 5-6

Sagittarius, the Bowman, 40
Saint Patrick's Day, xi, 50
Saranac Indians, 64-66
Scorpio, the Scorpion, 40

Scotchguard, 97
Sequins:
    harmonizing, 30
    placing on egg, 28-29
Silica sand, 10-12
Silver braid, 21
Silver leaf, 31, 99
Sizes (egg), 166-167
Suppliers, list of, 171-173

Table centerpiece, 7-8, 156
Taurus, the Bull, 39
Thanksgiving Day, 35
Thistle (symbol), 27
Tie-and-dye method, 5, 7
Time of day (in a goose egg), 141-143
Toothpick holders, eggs for, 150-151

Ukrainian Easter eggs, xiv
    how to decorate, 99-101

Valentine Day, ix
Valentine egg, 145-149
    interior of, 148-149
    motifs, 149
Velvet band, eggs on, 80-82
Victoria, Queen, 168
Virgo, the Virgin, 39

Water colors, 94
Water sprite, 155-157
Wax pencils, 5
Western eggs, leather-clad, 53-68
    beadwork, 60, 62, 67
    cowboy on horse, 60
    cutting and glueing, 53, 57, 60-61
    dyeing process, 57-58
    exterior rim, 61-62
    frame and stand, 61, 62
    Indian cradle design, 53-56
    interior rim, 61
    Kachina Doll, 62-64
        tribal legend design, 64-66
        tools for carving, 67-68
White House lawn, xiv

Zodiac eggs, 37-42
    correct color for, 40
    displaying, 40-42